# THE HALLMARKS FOR
# SUCCESSFUL BUSINESS

*For a complete list of Management 2000 titles
visit our website at www.mb2000.com*

# THE *NEW* HALLMARKS FOR SUCCESSFUL BUSINESS

## THE COMPLETELY REVISED AND UPDATED PRACTICAL GUIDE TO SUCCESSFUL BUSINESS DEVELOPMENT

### DAVID HALL & DINAH BENNETT

2000

First edition published 1992 by Management Books 2000

This new edition published 2000 by Management Books 2000 Ltd
Cowcombe House,
Cowcombe Hill,
Chalford,
Gloucestershire GL6 8HP
Tel: 01285-760722. Fax: 01285-760708
E-Mail: mb2000@compuserve.com

Printed and bound in Great Britain by Digital Books Logistics, Peterborough

British Library Cataloguing in Publication Data is available

ISBN 1-85252-274-7

# A Selection of What Hallmarks Companies Say

*"Hallmarks made me realise that you are always marketing your business, positively or negatively whether you realise it or not. Knowing this is half the battle."*
**Martin Rice, The Solution Design Consultants**

*"I found the Hallmarks programme the most stimulating and thought provoking programme I have undertaken. If we use the performance of the business as a measure of the success of Hallmarks then it has been an unqualified success – number of employees up from 26 in 1995 to 62 in 1999 and sales up from £1m to £2.5 m this year."*
**David Baker, ITEC North East**

*"Hallmarks has helped us transform the profitability of our business in ways which we could never have imagined."*
**Simon Keats, North Staffs Caravans.**

*"David Hall has been instrumental in the successful development of the Keepmoat Group over many years."*
**Dick Watson, Keepmoat Plc**

*"May I say thank you for your help over the years, we are off to the House of Commons to receive our award for the third year running – Unisys and Management Today awards for Customer Service."*
**Ann Adlington, Triple A Ranch**

*"The models and process have helped us improve our profitability every year for the past 3 years."*
**Martin Vincent, CompuAdd Computers**

*"David's idea about the key indicators has helped us get real control of the key aspects of our business and has made a big difference to our performance."*

**Alan Goodall, Danisco Pack (Chesterfield)**

*"The programme gave me some brilliant ideas based on tried and tested formulas for marketing products and helped me identify and focus on the type of business we needed to bring in."*

**Sue Allison, Dunhouse Quarry Co. Ltd**

# Contents

HALLMARK ('he:l,mg:k) n 1. A mark of authenticity or excellence. 2. An outstanding feature ~vb. 3. (tr) To stamp with as if a Hallmark (after Goldsmiths Hall in London).

# Preface

The original research for *The Hallmarks for Successful Business* was conducted in 1989/90 with the first edition being published in 1992. Since that time many hundreds of businesses have used the Hallmarks processes to help them to survive, change and grow.

The original book started with the objective of helping businesses to develop by passing on the experiences of successful business people. We now know that the entrepreneur's preferred way of learning is from successful peers so our original hunch turns out to have been correct.

In 1998 we had the idea of revisiting the 30 Hallmarks companies, that we originally researched 10 years ago, to find out what had happened to them and what new lessons they might have for other business people.

So what have they learned? What has affected them most? What new obstacles have they had to overcome? What has happened to them?

Our assumption was that we would need to adapt the original Hallmarks model in the light of our further investigations. It will be a relief to many to know that the basic structure and framework stays intact. The modules have been extensively used and have helped businesses to survive, change and grow. Our Hallmarks companies cautioned us about following the fad of creating something 'new' almost for its own sake; they were more interested in things that work well.

As a result of our investigations we have changed one Hallmark; Quality to Competitiveness. For that, we do not apologise. We should be just as committed to the continual improvement of our products and services as the best companies. In this second edition Dinah Bennett, the original researcher from the Foundation for SME Development at the University of Durham, joins me to scrutinise every page, paragraph and sentence in order to simplify the language, rework some of the methods, provide new examples and shorten the book. We have added some additional toolkits which companies have used and found helpful.

Our thanks once again to the Hallmarks companies and many others for allowing us access to their stories and wisdom.

# Aim

The aim of this book is:

1. *To help businesses survive, change or grow by passing on the Hallmarks for success from some successful businesses.*

In the first edition the aims were:

1. *To help businesses develop successfully, sustaining that development long-term.*

2. *To pass on Hallmarks for success from some successful businesses.*

3. *To provide practical ways of using these Hallmarks and add value to companies.*

4. *To enable support agencies to provide effective help to developing companies.*

As you can see, we have sought to make it easier by taking out as much waffle as we could!

# Introduction

## OVERVIEW

This introduction answers some questions you may be asking already:-

- What is this book about?
- Why was it written?
- How does this book work?
- What success and lessons have emerged from companies who have used the Hallmark ideas over the past 10 years?
- What is the role of the *translator*?

## What is this book about?

This book is about how successful independent companies with turnovers of up to £20 million develop and the lessons they learn in the process. These lessons are translated into practical step-by-step guidelines to enable you to achieve similar success. This book is about:

- *How to develop a continuously successful business.*
- *How to generate new business.*
- *How to position your business so that you can charge a premium price.*
- *How to create a sustainable competitive advantage.*
- *How to grow with minimum risk and sleep easily in your bed.*
- *How to ride the waves of boom and bust in the economy.*

- *How to become the recognised market leader.*
- *How to become the role model in your industry sector, i.e. 'the best'.*
- *How to develop other people so that the business is less dependent on you for its success.*

In this edition we have added a Hallmark to develop your business in the light of the tough economic conditions facing many companies in the late '90s.

## What It Is Not About...

It does not address production, personnel or finance issues. These are important areas for development but in my experience finding and keeping enough customers is the first and most important step to success.

With enough customers, these other areas can provide some nice problems for you to tackle next. The book is about business development through market and people development.

## Hallmarks not magic formulae

The book spells out some guiding Hallmarks for success. It does not provide a magic formula. Hallmarks need to be tailored to your business because the route to success depends upon your company's particular circumstances. Secondly, today's success formulae may have the opposite effect in a different environment tomorrow. Finally, each business needs to craft its own recipe for success.

Hallmarks then are the characteristic features consistently found in successful independent companies. These are not blueprints – you can't simply copy what others have done. You have to think out how you can use the ideas in your business. The Hallmarks contained in this book will help you by providing the basis for assessing, designing and running the business development aspects of your business.

# Why was the book written?

Because we have been working with your kind of company over the last twenty years and become dissatisfied with the support and help available to enable them to develop effectively.

- *In the UK, we need to produce more successful businesses, to maintain a healthy economy.*
- *Our entry into Europe and increasing global competition is exposing many UK businesses to aggressive competition which they are not prepared for.*

## What is the potential?

- *95% of all the radical innovation this Century has come from companies employing less than 20 people.*
- *Many independents find it hard to change or grow. Because they are keen to retain their independence they are reluctant to borrow or give up equity. Hardest of all is building the management team, delegating operational control and finding successors.*
- *Consequently, relatively few companies are consistently successful over a period of ten years or more.*

Amidst the welter of published advice on business success why is this book important?

- *Because most support for marketing and business development is based on big company models.*
- *Because business support tends to be administrative, for example how to write a business plan or construct a cash flow. The major problems however, are to do with getting orders, making customer contacts and meeting the right people.*

All this adds up to a mismatch of the needs of independent business and the type of support and help available.

We decided to find ways of helping these businesses more effectively. We asked ourselves:

- *How can we help independent businesses that want to survive, change or grow?*
- *What can be learnt from successful companies?*
- *Can we find some principles for success, which we confidently can pass on to others?*

This book tries to answer these questions.

## How this book works

The book is designed to give you choices about how you use it and what actions (if any) you decide to take.

Here is an overview of how the book works:

*Pages 7-20*    *Try to answer some of the important questions you may be considering before getting into the book, i.e. What is the book about? Is it right for me?*

*Pages 21-38*    *Help you to get the most out of the book by showing you how to gather information in order to assess your business against the Hallmarks.*

*This section also shows you a way to maximise the benefits you can get by reading this book – accelerating learning.*

*Pages 39-220*    *Show how to apply the Hallmarks to the development of your business. Each Hallmark is discussed at three levels, thus:*

| Level 1 | Awareness | You understand the process of successful development by reading the text and case studies |
|---------|-----------|-------------------------------------------------------------------------------------------|
| Level 2 | Assessment | You compare your business activities with the success factors using the framework provided |
| Level 3 | Action | You complete actions to develop your business. |

*You decide how far you want to go with factors you want to work on and to what level.*

Pages 221-265 contain 'toolkits' which enable you to work effectively with the Hallmarks. The Appendix describes our research aims and methodology.

*Toolkit 1*    *Developing a Customer Commitment – provides a framework to help your customer commitment to help your business. This provides a basis for moving on to delight customers.*

*Toolkit 2*    *Sets out exactly how to complete a Customer Perception Survey in order to find out how you are perceived by your customers. This provides the basis for developing your business.*

*Toolkit 3*    *Provides background reading to the process of problem-seeking/problem-solving to help you to really get to grips with the process which is the core of Successful Business Development. The benefits are that you will create more business opportunities than you can handle.*

*Toolkit 4*    *Outlines in detail a Business Generating System to ensure you have enough opportunities.*

*Toolkit 5*    *Searching for opportunities to improve competitiveness. This shows how to spot opportunities in a systematic way in order to stay ahead of your competitors.*

*Appendix*    *Details how the research with the 30 companies was conducted. This was a substantial research programme involving a full time researcher over two years.*

# Definitions of Words and Phrases Used in this Book

**Hallmarks:** *An outstanding feature of a successful business.*

**Independent Company:** *One which is privately owned with sales from £0.2m to £20m .*

**Successful Business:** *One which meets the following criteria:*

- *less than 10 years old and now employs 100+ people.*
- *maintained planned profit performance over the period of growth*
- *became recognised leaders in their market sector*

**Framework:** *A summary of the Hallmarks (outstanding features).*

**Accelerated Learning:** *Learning consciously to increase the quality and quantity of positive learning.*

**Customerising:** *Continually delighting customers.*

**Mission:** *The definition of the business you are in.*

**Vision:** *The future you want to create.*

**Core Skills:** *What you are really good at.*

**Networking:** *Working with those who can influence your business, e.g. Bank manager, sign-posters.*

**Customer Delight:** *Surprising customers by your level of service you provide to them personally.*

**'The Shadow Side':** *The things that do not get formally discussed in meetings, but have a big impact on your business, i.e. culture, politics, egos, etc.*

# What success and lessons have emerged from companies who have used the Hallmarks ideas over the past 10 years?

The Hallmarks models were turned into a franchised training and consulting business. Several hundred companies have been through Hallmarks programmes since 1993.

In 1997 John Lupton of Sheffield University conducted an independent review with 75 companies who had attended the programmes of the results they had achieved.

Here is a summary of the results:

**Business Generation**

| | |
|---|---|
| Revolutionised | 5% |
| Considerable improvement | 22% |
| Some improvement | 26% |

**Customer Commitment**

| | |
|---|---|
| Revolutionised | 5% |
| Considerable improvement | 17% |
| Some improvement | 41% |

**Profitability**

| | |
|---|---|
| Revolutionised | 4% |
| Considerable improvement | 31% |
| Some improvement | 30% |

**Idea Generation**

| | |
|---|---|
| Revolutionised | 3% |
| Considerable improvement | 31% |
| Some improvement | 30% |

The study also identified the major challenges facing those businesses:

- *The threats and opportunities of 'global' competition.*
- *Improving marketing techniques.*
- *Maintaining competitiveness.*
- *Obtaining and retaining 'quality' staff.*
- *Managing financial resources effectively.*
- *Managing organisation/technological change.*
- *The threats and opportunities caused by UK and EU legislation/ regulation.*
- *Achieving best business practice.*
- *Customer retention.*
- *Making time to work 'on' the business.*
- *Dealing with skill shortages among staff.*
- *Ever tighter margins reducing profit levels.*
- *Continuous innovation in terms of product development.*

The major conclusion of the independent research was that many of these issues are dealt with through the Hallmarks processes.

The issues not covered in the 1st edition of Hallmarks are dealt with in this 2nd edition by the inclusion of Hallmark 5: Competitiveness.

Dr Tim Mazzarol of Curtin Business School in Perth, Australia used the Hallmarks models to evaluate the performance of 88 businesses in Western Australia. He analysed their financial performance over a four-year period. His study "found a significant relationship between high sales growth and the following Hallmarks characteristics". In particular, he found:

- *A high level of environmental scanning.*
- *A greater control over their key resources.*
- *A stronger level of customer commitment.*
- *An organisational structure to support their business plan.*
- *A commitment to partnering with customers and suppliers.*
- *A strong commitment to ISO 9000 standards.*
- *A clear knowledge of critical information.*
- *Good cash-flow management.*
- *A commitment to taking action.*

The study also found that partnering was the highest correlation with success: *"The long term benefits of partnering as described in the Hallmarks book can be substantial."*

NatWest Business Managers and their Assistants have been trained at the University of Durham in the Hallmarks models, since 1992.

*"The programme aims to help bank managers to understand how small businesses really do survive, change and grow. The Hallmarks models provide a very helpful framework that banking people value because it helps them understand the business development process".*
### Robert Sentance, Nat West Programme Director, The Foundation at the University of Durham

The Hallmarks process has also been used by DUBS to teach entrepreneurs the process of business development in Romania, Australia and South Africa.

*"The models seem to make sense to business people across cultures. They value their practical, comprehensive yet simple way of communicating quite complex issues".*
### Dinah Bennett, The Foundation at the University of Durham

I (David Hall) have used the Hallmarks processes extensively in my consulting practice with entrepreneurial and large companies. I have learnt that when entrepreneurs make significant profit and business improvement gains then they nearly always follow a similar process:

1. *Develop a clear coherent shared strategy – (Hallmark 1).*
2. *Identify and remove the blockages to progress – (Hallmark 5).*
3. *Establish and monitor key indicators – (Hallmark 6).*
4. *Move from customer service to customer delight – (Hallmark 2).*
5. *Develop partnerships particularly with customer suppliers and staff – (Hallmark 3).*
6. *Develop a strong value set that holds the organisation together through both good and bad times – (Hallmark 4).*

This may not be a precise sequence of 1 to 6 as outlined in this book, but this is the way they do it in practice.

## What is the Role of the Translator?

In researching and developing Hallmarks we tried to adopt the role of translators. Translators try to stay in touch with the best of theory and research and the practical methods and processes that business people use in their everyday work. Sometimes walking the edge between theory and practice proves a problem. Academics accuse you of being too simplistic and not valid whilst hard-nosed business people accuse you of being too theoretical.

Our view is that the lack of translators, between good theories and proven practice, leads to the under-utilisation of some of our best business ideas.

Too often research into theories and into what really happens in practice is conducted separately. We believe that this is a mistake. Practice without theory is like man without reason, but theory without practice is self-indulgent, intellectual navel gazing.

# Introducing the Hallmarks for Success

## OVERVIEW

This book is based on information and learning from three major sources:

• It is based on research into 30 independent companies. Their experiences provide some Hallmarks for success. This section introduces you to these companies and provides an overview of their success routes. Key points are illustrated by examples from the experiences of these companies. Many of the quotations used are reproduced without alteration from recorded interviews.

• David Hall personal consultancy work using the Hallmarks with hundreds of businesses.

• Dinah Bennett's work, and that of her colleagues at The Foundation for SME Development at the University of Durham, using the Hallmarks models to train entrepreneurs, bank officials and the business support network.

## The Research Companies

The basis for selecting the businesses for the original research programme was:

•   *Small independent privately owned businesses*
•   *Turnover range £200,000 – £20m*
•   *Manufacturing and service sectors*
•   *Recognised successful companies*

80 companies which met the criteria were identified and contacted and 30 agreed to be involved in the research project. 26 are still trading 10 years later. One was sold for over £20m and three changed their trading names.

The principles of success come from their experiences. As they are the stars of the book they deserve to be credited here rather than hidden away in an appendix. The detailed research programme is outlined at Appendix 1.

| Company | Area of Operation |
|---|---|
| *NB Group* | *Print and Design* |
| *Topline* | *Business Services* |
| *Osborne Engineering* | *Manufacturer of White Metal Bearings* |
| *S.P.R* | *Maker of Video & TV Films* |
| *ABI Electronics* | *Electronic Test Equipment* |
| *Chameleon Design* | *Decorative Mirrors* |
| *Shield Engineering* | *Precision Tool Makers* |
| *Osborne Kay* | *Printers* |
| *Paul and Loughran* | *Gas Compressor Manufacturers* |
| *Canford Audio* | *Audio & Broadcasting Equipment* |
| *Tyne Tec* | *Access Control Equipment and Alarms* |
| *Panda* | *Protective Clothing & Equipment* |
| *Bede Scientific* | *'X' Ray Defraction Instruments* |
| *Fellowes* | *Manufacturer of Office Supplies* |
| *Polydon Industries* | *Production Engineering* |
| *Higgins* | *Potato Processing* |
| *Nicholson Seals* | *Gaskets and Seals* |
| *Neat Ideas* | *Office Supplies by Mail-order* |
| *Derwent Valley Foods* | *Snack Foods* |
| *Cresstale* | *Lipstick & Compact Containers* |
| *Bonas* | *Fabric Weaving Machines* |
| *Compass Caravans* | *Touring Caravans* |
| *Tolag* | *Components – Defence* |
| *Ace* | *Conveyor Systems* |
| *Elfab Hughs* | *Safety Equipment* |
| *Metro Fm* | *Broadcasting* |
| *Electrix Northern* | *Stainless steel equipment* |

Over the 10 years since the research was conducted for the first edition, on average the Hallmarks companies:

- *Increased sales by an average of 100%.*
- *Improved profits by an average of 300%.*
- *Increased number of employees by 92%.*

The major issues faced by our Hallmarks companies over the past 10 years can be summarised as:

- *'Coping with growth'*
- *'Getting everyone on board the vision'*
- *'Developing a management team capable of sustaining growth'*
- *'Improving weaknesses in management and systems'*
- *'Diversification's that failed'*
- *'Major customers going global'*
- *'Strong pound'*
- *'Increasing price competition from abroad'*
- *'Having to discount more to retain market share'*
- *'Reduced margins on core business'*
- *'Recruiting skilled enthusiastic employees'*

The major lessons Hallmarks businesses have learnt over the past 10 years can be summarised as:

- *'Teamwork is essential'*
- *'Do not be afraid of change'*
- *'Management style has to change'*
- *'Need for focus on specialised markets where we can compete'*
- *'Need to be in different sectors and play to our strengths'*
- *'Teams are paramount – shareholder harmony is key'*
- *'USP's vital to success – mass marketing is dead'*
- *'Developing new services is time consuming'*
- *'Trust and common goals are rare commodities'*
- *'IT and the Internet will change our business'*

# Findings

## *Hallmarks*

By analysing the successful companies we were able to develop a **Framework** for successful business development. The successful businesses all had what we have described as the six **"Hallmarks"** of success – from the dictionary definition of "Hallmark: *an outstanding feature*". These Hallmarks represent the basic principles for success for rapidly growing and successfully changing companies with a long-term future.

The business development Framework presents these six Hallmarks as an integrated model, with clear linkages between each part. Implementation of the model as a whole is the way to successful business development.

Each Hallmark has five steps to completion. The map below provides an overview and should help you find your way around the book.

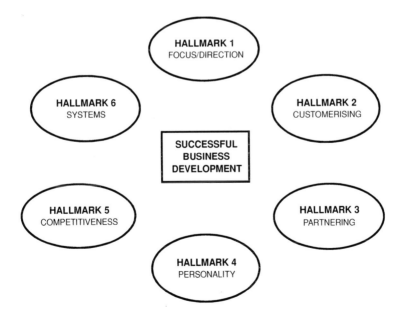

The Framework is a cycle, because:

- *The tasks to be completed are presented as a sequence (although you need to pay attention to them all at once). Start at twelve o'clock with Hallmark 1: **Focus/Direction** and work clockwise. Our research suggests there is a natural logical order to complete the tasks, which it is helpful to follow.*

  *For example, you cannot determine what critical resources are required until you have an overall view for the future.*

- *The tasks are obviously dependent on each other. For example Osborne Engineering used People to improve its personality (image) with its major customers.*

- *There is no such thing as completing the growth or change task. It is a constant journey.*

### Why Hallmarks?

The Hallmarks provide a model of managing which is missing in many businesses. They provide a shared model, which gives everyone in the business a road map enabling them to decide their priorities.

Hallmarks also helps you to plan and implement change. Many people and companies resist change out of fear. The Hallmarks provide a method of changing beliefs and making change an adventure.

The Hallmarks will help you develop your business providing you are ready to take management seriously.

# Hallmark 1

### *Focus/direction:* *Fashioning and managing the overall focus and direction of the business*

The successful companies all had clear focus and direction, which matched the business strengths with the opportunities in the market place and allowed their people to use their personal energies to the businesses benefit. Everybody was heading the same way. Yet few companies had written plans or strategies. It was more a sense of focus and direction was reinforced by the top team acting as role models for the business overall. This was particularly evident in *Derwent Valley Foods Metro FM.*and *Neat Ideas.*

# Hallmark 2

### *Customerising:     Continually delighting customers*

The successful companies without exception are committed to delighting their customers. Their method is such that we found difficulty in finding a word in the English language to describe it fully. Marketing for example was not descriptive enough. These companies focus on customers not markets. (In the history of business a market never bought anything). From top management down they identify with customers, sorting out their problems, providing fast effective solutions and building relationships. We felt the ideal process was not really captured by our vocabulary. Hence we coined the word CUSTOMERISING. Successful companies clearly define their core skills (what they are good at) and stick to them. They grow and develop by leveraging that strength with new customers often geographically, using a business generating system. *Cresstale, Compass* and *Ace* make solving customers problems in partnership a priority.

# Hallmark 3

### *Partnering:          Working in partnership with people*
### *who affect the business*

Working in partnership with all the key people who affect the business is a way of life for the successful companies. They treat their customers, staff, suppliers, and distributors as partners in their business. This is not a manipulative ploy but a genuine conviction that working in partnership is a way to succeed.

*Neat Ideas* fitted radios in the cabs of their distributors to help them improve communications. They also encourage their suppliers to join them in their in-company training programmes. *Derwent Valley Foods* have a company newspaper that is provided for customers, employees, suppliers and distributors.

## Hallmark 4

### *Personality:*      *The character of the business*

Commitment to a successful company image (external) is achieved though a carefully managed company personality (internal). Company personality is managed through a clear vision, which is communicated to everyone with the top management personally providing clear examples to follow.

Successful companies have the look and feel of success. They have a personality and vitality not seen in other businesses. Their external image is not left to chance. One Hallmark Company clearly defined company image down to colours worn in overalls and in the livery of their vehicles. This was one of its main attractions to its biggest customer British Telecom, because at the time British Telecom was trying to improve its image with its customers. They ran an advertising campaign emphasising the number of telephone boxes in working order. Their clear identity supported this aim.

## Hallmark 5

### *Competitiveness:*      *Building a sustainable competitive edge*

This is the new Hallmark we have added as a result of revisiting our original Hallmarks companies.

Many are facing crippling price and product competition much of it from overseas. The successful ones have responded by creating a sustainable competitive advantage.

*Derwent Valley Foods* has a quality product in superior packaging, which allows them to charge premium prices.

*Cresstale* focus on getting quality right for each individual customer.

*Neat Ideas* carries out spot checks on its carriers to ensure distribution meets their quality standards.

## Hallmark 6

### *Systems:*       *Establishing systems to provide information empowers people to make key decisions*

Some companies have clearly defined what they need to monitor and control to be successful. As well as being tightly controlled financially, they monitor key customer indicators using the information to make management decisions. The difference between ordinary businesses and the successful ones is that most successful companies provide information to empower people to act rather than control them.

*Neat Ideas* has reduced telephone ordering waiting time to 3 seconds. They take ACTION on the information rather than collect and store it.

If you are seriously interested in developing your business then you need to develop your capability. The rest of this book shows you how to do it. So far we have described the recipe for success: WHAT to do.

But how can you apply these findings to *your* business?

What can you do to successfully develop *your* business?

The following parts of the book take you through in a practical, step-by-step way, methods and means of developing your business: HOW to do it.

In order to use the Hallmarks you need information. This needs to be gathered in a systematic manner. The next section sets out how, from both inside and outside your business. The purpose of Section 3 is to TAKE THE FIRST STEP forwards in your business by creating information.

Section 3 also provides some tips to help you get the most out of the book. It explains our learning model and outlines what people who learn effectively actually do.

# The first step

## OVERVIEW

In order to complete the Hallmarks for your business you need to gather information and take action. This Section offers some practical tips about using the book, gathering information in order to assess your business and how to take actions to develop. The learning model is explained in depth.

| Development Model | Outcome |
|---|---|
| 1. *Awareness* | *Understanding of the process of Successful Business Development* |
| 2. *Assessment* | *Assess your business against the Hallmarks* |
| 3. *Action* | *Actions taken to develop your business* |

## Level 1:   Awareness

**Awareness** is a basic understanding of how the growth businesses achieved success. In creating awareness we have deliberately kept theory and jargon out and tried to encourage the successful companies to paint pictures for you by telling their own stories. When you read each awareness section try to relate the experience of others to your business. How could we do that? Could we make that work for us? Talk to your colleagues about the examples. Look out for your own examples. Try to understand your business through the Hallmarks outlined. For example, how effective is our networking?

Don't just passively read the examples, but try to fit them into your world. In this way you will start to develop your business.

# Level 2: Assessment

The purpose of this level is to encourage you to assess and learn more about your own business and its potential.

It provides a process to enable you to complete all the assessment sections in this book.

One of the difficulties in assessing your own business is that you are often too close to it and can't see the wood for the trees. As one businessman said recently, "Don't confuse me with the facts, I have made my mind up already!"... If you are to develop your business you need an objective assessment of current reality: facts not opinions, specifics not generalities, solid information not myths or fantasy.

In order to gather factual information this Section helps you with some key questions. Try to answer them as honestly as possible, there is no point doing a P.R. job on yourself!

There are two major sources of information to enable you to assess your business objectively.

**Internal** – *Management colleagues and staff*
**External** – *Customers*

## Internal

When completing the assessment sections it will help if you ask people inside your business to answer the questions. Assemble your top team and put the questions to them to answer. Ask your network for their views. Try to stay open minded, you may not like all the answers you get. If all you want to hear is that you are wonderful then perhaps you should not undertake the exercise. Most businesses have strengths and weaknesses; you undoubtedly will be the same.

The purpose of asking other people is to enable you to identify your own particular blind spots.

To help you obtain some objective feedback internally the assessment sections of the book can be photocopied and you can ask your people to complete them. You can also complete it. You can then assess and compare your ratings with your people. You are strongly recommended to take this step. For example:

- *Do your scores differ from your company directors?*

- *Are there different scores at different levels in the business.*

- *Which Hallmarks are strengths (high scores) and which are weaknesses (low scores).*

This information is vital if you are going to take positive action to develop your business.

Remember, internally, people will tell you (if you are the boss) what they think you want to hear. Good news upwards is normal. A good probing question to ask is "Thank you for that information, now tell me what you really think?". You often need to dig deeper to get closer to current reality.

Make a note of the responses you get. If you ask enough people and dig deep enough you will get a clear picture of the reality of your business. You can then move forward and develop.

## External

Every business I know says they know and understand their customers. "We are dealing with them every day". This presents a problem in gathering objective information. A businessman said to me recently when questioned about the quality of their Customerising, "We must be OK, we don't get many complaints." Frankly if your customer service is based on complaints then sell the business today! Very often you and I are so close we can't see the real picture. It can be helpful to stand back and undertake a systematic review of customer's perception of your business.

The way to do this is to complete a customer perception survey. Exactly how this should be completed is laid out step-by-step as Toolkit 1. This information will enable you to assess your business objectively and develop it successfully. Again, you are strongly recommended to take this step. Your competitors won't so you have the basis of competitive advantage – better information on customers.

# Level 3: Action

Action either brings success or learning. Successful companies get into action quickly and do not suffer paralysis by analysis. This section seeks to encourage you to try things out, experiment, and have a go. It includes tips and ideas in order to develop your business. It also includes step by step actions to take to encourage you to have a go. **Learning takes place when options are increased.** This book aims to deliberately increase your options. Here are some things that learners seem to do:

**Learners:**

- *Go at risk – they have a go, try new ideas*
- *Are prepared to be wrong – no one can be right all the time. If we are to learn then we need to let go of the past and admit we were wrong.*
- *Ask questions – learners are always asking questions. Why did that happen? How does it work? How can we improve?*
- *Tolerate ambiguity – there are no 'right' answers in business. If there were we would all be multimillionaires! Learners recognise that business is about opportunities and percentages.*
- *Do not take themselves too seriously – business is serious but it can be fun and when it is fun we seem to make progress.*
- *Are optimistic – optimism rubs off on others, it builds energy and commitment.*

Conversely non-learners also seem to do certain things.

- *Stay quiet – they never take risks, never get involved. They may be cynical and quietly arrogant.*
  *(Definition of a cynic – somebody who has given up but not shutup!)*
- *Want definitive answers – non-learners want the magic key: "Tell me what to do to make a million..."*
- *Rationalise – "Yes, but..." "It won't work here because..." "We tried it once..." "Our business is different..." You know the syndrome!*
- *Quote past precedents (normally out of context) – "We tried that*

*20 years ago and...” “I selected Fred and he's a star” (they forget to tell you about the other 20 they “selected” who have since been sacked).*

• 	Are pessimistic – "The recession..." "The Japanese..." "It won't work..." "There's no point trying..."

This could be summarised by:

**Learners** 	= 	**open minded**
**Non-Learners** = 	**closed minded**

One thing is clear, no one can teach you anything. You decide whether you want to learn. It is your responsibility, not mine. The goods can be put on display in the shop window, but you must decide whether to buy...

1.1
Mission

1.5
Key resources

1.2
Vision

**HALLMARK 1:
Focus/direction**

1.4
Environment

1.3
Core skills

# Hallmark 1 – Focus/direction

## OVERVIEW

Successful companies share many common features although each one creates its own recipe for success.

One common feature is clear focus and direction. This enables people to harness their personal energies and to add value to the business. This Section outlines the key principles involved in the process of fashioning and managing overall focus and direction.

*Hallmark 1:*     *Focus/Direction provides an overview of the key principles involved in the process. The key is to ensure that each factor on the Hallmark supports the others – e.g., what key resources do we require to deliver the vision? Or, how can we use our core skills to satisfy our customers needs?*

The same principles apply as those outlined with the original framework for business development. Here is a reminder:

* *These are principles, not magic formulae.*
* *These principles are sequential. Start with Mission and work clockwise round the Hallmark. You will find that there is a logical sequence from 1 to 5. You really need to complete 1 before 2 and 2 before 3, etc.*

In the late 1990s, one way of revitalising businesses is to re-do your strategy focusing on areas where you make money and exiting loss-making parts of your business.

# ...AWARENESS

## 1.1 Mission

### – What business are we in?

One of the apparently easiest yet in practice most difficult business questions to answer is – What business are we really in? This has been called the mission of the business.

Here are some examples of missions:

| | |
|---|---|
| *AbleClean:* | *Quality Cleaning For the North East* |
| *Derwent Valley Foods:* | *Quality Adult Snack foods* |
| *Darfen:* | *Security Systems* |
| *Neat Ideas:* | *Mail Order Office Products* |

The purpose of a mission is to draw a boundary round the scope of the business: to define the business clearly and communicate it to people so they can use it as a framework for decision making and to add value. These missions differ from the classical statements normally associated with large companies in that they are shorter and do not attempt to be all encompassing. They serve to describe the business in a simple way.

Here are some guidelines:

1. *A powerful mission statement is short, clear and simple. It has between 6-10 words. It rolls off people's tongues.*
2. *It states clearly what business you are in.*
3. *It avoids generalities.*
4. *It focuses on what the organisation is now rather than what it might be in the future.*

39

Developing a mission provides a good illustration of how Hallmarks work in practice. In order to determine what business you are in you need to consider what are you good at (core skills) and what opportunities exist for you (environment). You need to work around the Hallmark in order to craft an effective mission. This highlights the interdependence of the principles in the Hallmark model.

In our success companies we noted that:

1. *They had a mission that was communicated from the top.*
2. *Management actions reinforce the mission. The decisions they take, the questions they ask, the issue or agendas.*
3. *People do not argue about the mission, only how they can add value to it.*
4. *The best missions motivate people, they want to contribute to a greater good.*

## So what is your mission?

Some companies have re-invented themselves by redoing their strategy; *ABI Electronics* is a good example. They were local business heroes in the late 1980s Winning my prestigious business award, Alison Fletcher told me:

> *"We thought we had the right to be successful and we took our eye off the ball. It nearly cost us our business. We have now refocused and are doing well once again."*

Do you need to refocus your business?

# ...ASSESSMENT

## 1.1   Mission

**Tick here if this is true
for your business:**

1. *We have a clearly articulated mission that fits
   the criteria for mission established in this Section.*   ☐

2. *We use our mission to provide focus for our
   business decisions.*   ☐

3. *Our mission describes accurately our true identity
   and what we are about.*   ☐

4. *Everyone in our business understands our mission.*   ☐

5. *Our people behave in line with the spirit of the
   mission.*   ☐

6. *Our people find it easy to contribute to our mission.*   ☐

If you can honestly tick all six questions you have a clear mission that
is driving your business. You might want to move onto other parts of
our framework. Less than four ticks, and you might decide to improve
your Focus/Direction by moving onto the next section, **ACTION**.

This aims to help you take action to improve your business, to
translate knowledge into a profitable improvement to your business.

# ...ACTION

## 1.1 Mission

Select any action you want to take to develop your business. This might be as a result of the assessment, feedback from your people or preferably your Customer Perception Survey.

**Action 1**     If you already have a mission statement ask yourself these key questions and take ACTION on the answers:

- *Does it meet the criteria set out in our Awareness section?*
- *Who knows about it?*
- *Do we really use it to make decisions?*
- *Do we need to shape it up?*

**Action 2**     If you do not have a mission then consider developing one.

Answer the question, What business are we really in?, by:

A. *Looking historically at where you have made money on projects, products or services?*
B. *Assessing opportunities in your environment. What opportunities exist for your business?*

Combine the answers to the questions in A and B together to make C – your mission.This is the essence of strategic thinking; the process of synthesis – bringing together – as opposed to analysis, which is breaking down into parts.

**Action 3**    Publish your mission.

- *Put it on the back of your business cards.*
- *Put it upon a sign in reception.*
- *Add it to your letterheads and stationery.*
- *Talk about it to your people.*

**Action 4**    Re-do your Strategy.

Many of the businesses we surveyed in our original research have had to reinvent themselves by redoing their strategy. Take a time-out to rethink your strategy and refocus your business on areas of real opportunity.

**...AWARENESS**

1.2
Vision

## 1.2   Vision

### – Spelling out the future you want

Vision is about having some idea of the kind of future we want and committing ourselves to getting there. This may not be simply in terms of making a million pounds in five years – vision is often much broader. In fact, not one of our success companies set out to make a million!

The problem for most of us is that the simple question: What do we really want? is very difficult to answer. Goal clarification is a lifelong process. It is about growing up and maturing. At the point of clarifying your goals, try to stop worrying about how you will get there. If the goals are important enough, you will invent ways to achieve them.

One company Chairman told us, "We can't predict the future in our industry, so we don't try. We just invent it."

If we then consider our present business and are dissatisfied, we move towards the new vision. You were encouraged to complete a Customer Perception Survey earlier in this book. Hopefully it triggered some actions to improve and move towards the picture you have of your business – how you would like it to be.

Vision creates new standards for your future. It could include:

*   *Where will we be positioned in the industry/market?*
*   *Whom will we be doing business with?*
*   *What will our customers say about us?*
*   *What lifestyle will I have?*

Vision is about creating a clear picture of the future that you want to create for yourself and your business, then working out goals for your business.

The next stage is to communicate that vision to energise and motivate the people to want to be part of your vision.

The key job of any leader is to create a vision and sell it to the people. You are a powerful role model whether you like it or not!

---

## *Example:–*

One of my customers was considering developing a new vision with the management team. However, the consensus in the team was that they were not ready for it because the Chief Executive was trapped in history – last month's accounts. All his questions were about the past. All his focus seemed to be on how did we do last month? There was never any discussion about the future. The message to the team was to forget the future, yesterday is what matters. He presented the wrong message to his people.

---

Vision is about stretching out and taking a big leap. It is not about business planning, the definition of which in many businesses seems to be last year's sales plus 10% plus hope!

A key message in this book is that the limiting factor on growth of your business is not funds, time, people, the government, interest rates or the next door neighbour's dog, the limiting factor is *your vision*! If your vision is powerful enough and people are committed to it, YOU WILL INVENT THE WAY. You will solve problems, find resources, make contacts, obtain finance and get there. So how far out can your vision be?

Remember, it is up to you. It is fine to have a vision that is last year's sales plus 10%, if that is what you really want. We are not all the same. Some want to conquer the world, others want to reduce their golf handicap to scratch.

So to be successful we need two things:

1. *Clearly state what future we want –* **Vision.**
2. *Get our team behind us in moving towards our vision –* **Teamwork.**

You don't need to know how you are going to achieve your vision, but the point is that at this stage you don't have to. All you need is the belief you can do it, and you may well succeed. This is fundamental because it creates the energy – the driving force. It is about faith, belief without evidence. There can be no facts about the future, only belief.

This illustration indicates another key point. When we arrive at our destination, our energy shuts down. We become blasé and complacent – bored with success. Therefore we need to renew our vision, otherwise we just disappear...

A key job of the top management of any business is to create the future vision and communicate it to people. Once we get a critical mass of people behind us, then anything is possible. That's your job.

---

### Example:–

My employer was not doing his customers any favours, it was all done on the cheap. I decided to do it and supply the quality the customer was after. I wanted to bring real quality into the cleaning business. My vision was all about quality. It worked and we doubled the price.

**- A Hallmark Company**

---

### Example:–

Panda Supplies hold joint meetings with customers, suppliers and staff to keep them updated on the on the company's progress. They make it fun and enjoyable so people want to attend.

---

# ...ASSESSMENT

## 1.2   Vision

Tick if this is true for your business

1. *We have a clear vision for our future.* ☐

2. *We communicate our vision to our people at every possible opportunity.* ☐

3. *Our vision energises and provides an incentive for everyone in our business.* ☐

4. *We seem to find ways of moving towards our vision* ☐

5. *There is something in our vision for customers, staff and investors.* ☐

6. *We are future focused rather than being trapped by history (or how things used to be).* ☐

Less than 4 ticks and you need to take ACTION.

# ...ACTION

## 1.2   Vision

**Action 5**   Take your top team away for two days. Talk about the future you want to create. Craft a vision for the future that involves your team in the process. Here is how to do it.

*Step 1:* *Put the question to your team. In three years:*
- *Whom do we really want to do business with?*
- *How should we treat our people?*
- *What style do we want to have?*
- *Where will we be positioned in the industry?*

*Step 2:* *Get them to write down answers to these questions.*

*Step 3:* *Discuss each other's answers. Debate them until you get common agreement and commitment to your future.*

*Step 4:* *Publish the results to everyone.*

**Action 6**   Take every opportunity to discuss your vision with your people. Don't assume they know or have thought about it. That's your job. Once they have clear direction they will search for ways to make it happen. 20 people focused on achieving your vision have to be better than one.

**Action 7**   Talk to suppliers, customers, your network, about your vision. They will help you. You will be amazed.

**Action 8**   Create a vision that seems too big, e.g. work in USA! Small visions do not motivate anybody.

# ...AWARENESS

1.3
Core skills

## 1.3   Core Skills

### – *What you are fundamentally good at*

> ## *Example:*
>
> *Keepmoat*, which operates in the construction industry, analysed historically which type of work had been most profitable for them. Over 20 years they had consistently made money on refurbishment contracts (smartening up council houses), building new houses and design/build contracts. They either made or lost money on almost everything else, but in an unpredictable way. They decided to stick to these areas of core skillthey had identified.
>
> In five years, they quadrupled their sales and profits. They became the 11th best performing UK business out of 10,000 in a national survey, coming from nowhere. Yet the middle managers wanted to employ their creativity by taking on more "exciting projects" (exciting for whom?). They were bored with making lots of money...!

This example illustrates some of the key issues when focusing on core skills:

- *Work out carefully what you are good at. This may be narrower than you think. In our example, they were consistently successful in only three core skill areas.*
- *Core skills are developed over time normally as a result of a lot of problem-solving (learning).and accumulated know-how.*

*49*

- *Core skills are product- or process-development on the job – skills are developed with customers. They are usually crafted from experience.*

The example also highlights an interesting paradox of focusing on core skills. Often the things that make us money are those we also find boring. We want to create some excitement in our lives, so we diversify – and screw up! Tom Peters in his Excellence books tells companies to 'stick to the knitting'– do what you are good at. This seems to fit with our success companies' experiences.

*Ace Conveyors* have considerable engineering expertise yet they focus on supplying and maintaining conveyors because that is what they are good at – "our core skills are in conveyors".

We learned two more important lessons from our companies:

1. *Not only do companies get bored with their core product/service skills, they also can grow bored with their business generating method. The top management may get business, say, by visiting customers or attending trade fairs. They get fed up with this mode and sales drop. They then panic and throw money at an advertising campaign – the wrong promotion channel. It fails. Successful companies 'stick to the knitting' not only in products but also with their primary business generating method. So if it works, don't knock it!*

2. *Core skills are those which are defined by your customers and not you. This is a crucial point. One company thought their competitive advantage was the quality of reports they produced. However, a survey revealed that their customers perceived the quality of their reports to be similar to that of their competitors, they had no real competitive advantage. However, customers did perceive that they had a competitive advantage through the quality of the relationships they established with them. Once the consultancy firm was aware of this competitive advantage they could try to leverage it into developing new business. So competitive advantage can be seen as a set of core skills unique to a business.*

## Example:–

When we were first set up we made anything and everything, we were fighting for business, and anything that was plastic we tried. Then we looked at what we were good at and what the market really wanted and decided to focus on lipstick containers and compacts. Now 60% of our business is in lipstick containers, 40% in compacts. We took off when we decided to focus on what were good at.....

*– Cresstale*

# ...ASSESSMENT

## 1.3    Core Skills

**Tick here if this is true
for your business:**

1. *Our core skills are clearly defined, we stick to
   them at all times.*                                      ☐

2. *We are constantly trying to nourish and expand
   our core skills.*                                        ☐

3. *Our customers confirm our own view of our core
   skills.*                                                 ☐

4. *We are good at using our core skills to create new
   opportunities.*                                          ☐

5. *Our core skills provide us with competitive
   advantage.*                                              ☐

6. *Our core skills support our vision.*                    ☐

Less than 4 ticks and you need to take **ACTION...**

# ...ACTION

## 1.3   Core Skills

**Action 9**     Assess historically where you make money: Which products, projects or services? Stick to these in the future or widen the way in which they can be used.

**Action 10**     Assess how you get business effectively? Is it face to face, exhibitions mailshots? Stick to the proven method in the future.

**Action 11**     Decide how you can exert leverage from your core skills and build your business. One training organisation's activity was teaching presentation skills to groups on training programmes. Having confirmed this as a core skill they decided to use it themselves to build their business by attending and speaking at conferences which trainers attended, to sell their services. They doubled their size in six months.

**Action 12**     Update your core skills continuously. Do not expect your competitors to play fair. They will try to chip away at your advantages. You need to keep your skills up-to-date and ahead of your competitors.

Here are some ideas to help you achieve this aim:

- *Who are the best in the business. What do they do? (This is called benchmarking.)*
- *Your upgrading of core skills will inevitably at some point include the use of I.T. at some point. Discuss with an I.T. specialist how you can develop your business.*

- *Visit a foreign country: USA, France, Japan on a Trade visit via your Chamber of Commerce or DTI.*
- *Challenge your people. Make it an adventure. Put it on the agenda: How can we develop our core skills?*
- *Read **'Kaizen': The Key to Japan's Competitive Success** by Masaaki Imai (Published by: McGraw-Hill Publishing Co, Maidenhead, December 1989).*

# ...AWARENESS

1.4
Environment

# 1.4   Environment

## – *Scanning the environment for threats and opportunities*

Our successful companies had business plans with clearly defined missions, visions and objectives. This did not stop them from acting opportunistically. Growth appears to come as a result of getting organised to identify and take opportunities. Growth is seen as a series of projects (opportunities) rather than a grand scheme or detailed blue-print. These findings are in line with much of the research into growth companies conducted by Durham University Business School.

Scanning the environment for opportunities and threats consists of three steps:

1. *Developing a 'culture of vigilance' to identify threats and opportunities.*
2. *Analysing the information gathered.*
3. *Developing projects to take up opportunities or guard against threats.*

In order to scan the environment successful companies stay close to the action and network with people. This provides information about threats and opportunities. An environmental map may assist the process. This can help to see the world more clearly and get rid of some blind spots. Such a map consists of questions to ask in key areas:

• *What is the government going to do that might affect our business?*
• *How will the changes in the economy affect us?*

55

- *What are the industry trends?*
- *What are our competitors up to?*

Each company needs to develop its own map in order to track the environment for opportunities and threats.

The major changes in the environment that have affected our Hallmarks companies over the past 10 years can be summarised as follows:

## Deregulation and the breakdown of national trading boundaries

Increased global competition has exposed many of our businesses to both threats and opportunities. On balance the effect has been negative. Cheap imports from countries with low wage costs have really threatened UK manufactures. *Polydon Industries* for example who manufacture parts for tractors and farm spraying equipment currently face a major threat to their core business from cheap Turkish imports.

Globalisation may be an opportunity for blue chip companies, but it has been a nightmare for many smaller businesses.

## Adverse currency exchange rates

Many Hallmarks companies have suffered 30-40% price disadvantage over the past 3 years due to adverse currency exchange rates.

## Increased price and service competition

Many companies are struggling in markets where supply exceeds demand; over capacity being a constant reality, trying to remain competitive in the face of significant volume reductions at the same time as 20-30% price reductions. How can they cope? This new phenomenon of the late '90s is addressed in the book by creating a new chapter, 'Hallmarks: Competitiveness' that examines these problems.

## Increased red tape and regulations

There has been a massive increase in red tape over the past ten years with successive UK governments believing it knows best and needs to legislate for almost every aspect of business life. Financial penalties have also increased dramatically. One example: unfair dismissal can now cost small businesses £50k (used to be £12k).

## Growth of communications technology

The growth of the Internet and the potential of e-commerce has created new opportunities for businesses. We met one self-employed cake maker in the North East who exports 80% of her products to the USA with the help of DHL and the Internet.

In summary, the last ten years' changes in the business environment have caused more problems than they have created new opportunities for Hallmarks companies. We try to help deal with some of those issues in the rest of this book.

# ...ASSESSMENT

## 1.4   Environment

**Tick here if this is true
for your business**

1. *We are very effective at scanning our business environment.*     ❏

2. *We are constantly identifying threats and opportunities to our business.*     ❏

3. *We have created more opportunities than we can handle.*     ❏

4. *We have effective intelligence gathering systems.*     ❏

5. *We are rarely taken by surprise by our business environment.*     ❏

6. *We feel we manage rather than being managed by our environment.*     ❏

Less than 4 ticks and you need to take **ACTION...**

# ...ACTION

## 1.4   Environment

**Action 13**   Create an environment map to assist you in the process of monitoring your environment.

*Step 1: Use the checklist to identify those areas that affect your business.*

- *Customer needs*
- *Government*
- *Local Government*
- *Government Agencies*
- *Economy*
- *Political Climate*
- *Competitors*
- *Changing Demographics*
- *Industry Trends*
- *Technology*
- *International Events*

*Include your own factors.*

*Step 2: Use the map frequently to scan your business environment for threats and opportunities.*

*Step 3: Report the key issues at management meetings.*

**Action 14**   Ask your trade body for reports on the business environment.

**Action 15**   Read the new Competitiveness (Hallmarks 5) for help in dealing with the changing environment.

**Action 16**   Stay close to your main contacts. Develop a 'culture of vigilance' towards your business contacts.

**Action 17**   Talk to anybody who can help your business who wants to visit you.

**Action 18**   Attend as many free business presentations in your area as you can, in the evenings or even at breakfast time. Talk to people.

**...AWARENESS**

1.5
Key resources

## 1.5   Key Resources

### – Identify and maintain a supply of key resources

Some resources are essential if your business is to succeed. Some key
resources may be readily available, while others may need organising.
Key resources are those that enable you to do business effectively.
These may include.

**Money**              *Access to capital and funds for growth.*

**Materials**          *Basic raw materials may require planning and
                       managing, particularly if they are in short supply.*

**People**             *Lack of people resources is often the limiting
                       factor in the development of a successful business.*

**Technology**         *Do you have the right technology to compete?*

**Brain Power**        *Do you have creative ideas or problem-solving
                       abilities.*

**Information**        *A critical resource today.*

**Contacts/Network**   *Contacts are a key resource in the development
                       of any business.*

**Customer Base**      *Is it large enough and well defined?*

**Image**              *Can create business for you if it is positive.*

Availability of herbs and spices that only grow in certain climates is a
key resource for *Derwent Valley Foods.*

Vehicles are essential to enable another Hallmark Company to do their work in cleaning telephone boxes. They are a key resource. Funding was a problem, sixteen banks said 'no' to lending the money but the seventeenth agreed.

The distribution network is a key resource for *Neat Ideas*, enabling them to achieve a 90% customer service level on delivery – on time.

Key resources control your move towards your vision.

---

"Our key resources are our contacts in Eastern Europe. We know whom to talk with to develop our business. Without these resources we could not operate effectively and certainly could not develop our business."

**- Chameleon Design**

---

Developing businesses often need access to capital. They also need effective people to drive the business forward. Access to information can be a critical resource. If I understand my customer's real needs better than my competitors do, I can exploit this opportunity.

In summary, key resources support vision, but so does every other principle in this Hallmark.

**Focus** and **Direction** come from thinking through these long-term issues and ensuring that all the principles support each other in an integrated way.

## ...ASSESSMENT

## 1.5    Key Resources

**Tick here if this is true
for your business**

1.  *We have identified and ensured we have a
    regular supply of key resources.*    ❑

2.  *Our key resources support the focus and direction
    of our business.*    ❑

3.  *Our business will not be stifled by the lack of key
    resources in the future.*    ❑

4.  *We have made plans to ensure a continuous supply
    of key resources.*    ❑

5.  *Our people resource is well managed and adds real
    value to our business.*    ❑

Less than 4 ticks and you need to take **ACTION...**

## ...ACTION

## 1.5   Key Resources

*Action 19:*   Identify your key resources required to achieve your
objectives.

*Step 1: List your vision and customer needs.*

*Step 2: Assess key resources required to meet Step 1
using the following checklist:*

| | Tick those important to your business | Tick those with whom you have an effective supply |
|---|---|---|
| | **A** | **B** |
| *People* | ❏ | ❏ |
| *Materials* | ❏ | ❏ |
| *Energy* | ❏ | ❏ |
| *Information* | ❏ | ❏ |
| *Technology* | ❏ | ❏ |
| *Capital* | ❏ | ❏ |
| *Natural Resources* | ❏ | ❏ |
| *Contacts* | ❏ | ❏ |
| *Partners* | ❏ | ❏ |
| *Others* | ❏ | ❏ |

*Step 3: Assess your current resources and plan your
future supply by considering the gaps
between A and B.*

*Action 20*   Get an independent person/body to assess the
quality of your key resources.

*Action 21*   Consider your people resources. Are they good enough
to deliver your vision? What development do they
need? Talk to your local Business Link about
Development programmes such as Investors in People.

2.1
Developing
a customer
commitment

2.5
Market
development

**HALLMARK 2:
Customerising**

2.2
Networking

2.4
Customer
delight

2.3
Problem-seeking
Problem-solving

# Hallmark 2 – Customerising

## OVERVIEW

**Total customer commitment = Customerising.**

**This chapter shows how to systematically customerise the business through awareness, assessment and action.**

**Customerising is a distillation from our research of the way successful companies stay close to customers, seek and solve their problems, creating customer delight.**

*Hallmark 2:*     *Customerising provides an overview of the key principles involved in the process.*

The process of customerising focuses resources onto customer contact on an ongoing basis. Some people have called this relationship marketing. Successful companies seek out important customers and spend considerable time helping them solve problems. They develop skills in a specific area sharpening and shaping those skills over time. They go out of their way to delight customers by providing that bit extra. None of our success companies employ formal marketing methods. Hence we invented customerising.

## ...AWARENESS

**2.1 Developing a customer commitment**

# 2.1   Developing customer commitment

How can you develop a customer commitment? What experiences shape this commitment?

In the case of one Hallmark Company the owner had previously worked for British Telecom and was dissatisfied with the quality of cleaning services provided. He decided to set up in business 'to do it better', supplying cleaning services to British Telecom. He developed his customer commitment from the experiences of being on the receiving end. The school of experience.

*Derwent Valley Foods'* management team worked in the snack food business. They spotted opportunities to serve customers better so they set up their own operation.

In other cases customer commitment is developed by staying close to customers, listening, identifying and responding to their needs. *Ace Conveyors'* 24-hour customer service policy evolved from solving customer problems. Problem-solving is learning.

In every case the key people set the standard and created the examples for others in their company to follow. One owner manager put it well:

*"In every decision we ask the question – What value will this add to our customers business? If our answer is positive we do it. Everybody in our business recognises it is not the geniuses in the boardroom who pay the wages, it's our customers."*

This attitude should be the norm, but unfortunately in our experience it is the exception. In *Metro FM's* car park, spaces for customers are conveniently near to reception. In many businesses the convenient car parks are reserved for directors.

These are simple examples but they indicate clearly an attitude of mind towards customers. It is the little things that count. Here is an example:

---

## *Example:*

I visited one of the Hallmarks research companies for the first time. The security guard at the gate knew my name and asked me to park next to Reception. The receptionist greeted me by name (how?) and asked me to take a seat while she filled in the visitors' book on my behalf. Ten seconds after I was seated a lady appeared with a black coffee in a nice china cup. (How did she know that is what I wanted without asking?). A P.A. arrived and informed me my contact would be with me in 2 1/2 minutes. At the stroke of 10.30 she emerged, greeted me warmly and escorted me to her office. I didn't need to see their accounts to know this company was successful.....

At another of the research companies the following day, the security guard wandered over, sighed deeply, and informed me there was a public car park half a mile away. Eventually I arrived at Reception, where I was requested to fill in a book. The receptionist sniffed at me, looked me up and down (he obviously thought I was selling double-glazing) and told me to wait. I found a coffee machine with paper cups. After being kept waiting 20 minutes I was ushered into a small meeting room. I didn't need to see their accounts, either....

---

How do you get customer commitment? It starts at the top. It is your job to set the example. You cannot delegate the responsibility.

## *Example:–*

A young man who could not read or write joined our business start-up programme at Chesterfield. He wanted to start a roof tiling business. He placed a small advert in the local paper. He installed a telephone answer machine at home and went about his business. When he arrived home and before sitting down to dinner he played all his messages back and rang potential enquiries. He then visited them immediately and gave them a quote. Only then did he return home for dinner. He understood the need to respond quickly to customers and as a result has a full order book.

# ...ASSESSMENT

## 2.1 Developing Customer Commitment

Using the information gathered internally and externally answer the questions as objectively as you can.

**Tick here if this is true**
**for your business**

1. *Customers find it easy to buy from us.*  ❑

2. *We do not employ any sales prevention officers here.*  ❑

3. *Top management set high standards for customer commitment.*  ❑

4. *We are committed to understanding the differences between our customers needs and wants.*  ❑

5. *We can provide six good examples of our commitment to customers from our last months activity.*  ❑

6. *Customer commitment is a way of life in our business.*  ❑

Less than four ticks and you might decide to improve your Customerising by moving onto the next section **ACTION.**

# ...ACTION

## 2.1   Developing customer commitment

This is the ACTION sequence:

*Action 22*   If you haven't already then conduct a detailed Customer Perception Survey along the lines outlined in Toolkit 1 to assess your current level of customer commitment.

*Action 23*   Take any aspect of your business (preferably one that has been identified by your Customer Perception Survey) and improve it. Set yourself an objective to achieve this month; e.g.:

- *Cut delivery lead-time by 1 week.*
- *Quote within 48 hours rather than 1 week.*
- *Contact all key customers at least once by telephone this month.*

*Action 24*   Ask your key customers this question over the next month:

*"How easy are we to buy from?"*

Act on the results.

*Action 25*   Set one example to your business of customer commitment that is highly visible this week; e.g.:

- *Personally deliver or return an important quotation by hand the same day.*
- *Put a system in place to record how customers who visit take their refreshments. Make it an automatic process to surprise them.*

**Action 26**   Visit a key customer to learn more about their business rather than sell them your product.

**Action 27**   Invite a customer to visit your premises to learn more about your business.

**Action 28**   Occasionally hand write a short personal note on letters to your customers.

**Action 29**   Call the customers regularly to talk to them.

**Action 30**   E-mail customers with snippets of information.

**Action 31**   Pass on copies of articles/information intelligence to customers.

**Action 32**   Place a customer welcome board in reception and keep it updated. An ad agency in Birmingham uses an old PC to give an 'electronic' welcome.

# ...AWARENESS

## 2.2 Networking

### – Working with those who can influence your business

There are many people who can influence the performance of your business. The obvious ones are customers, suppliers, employees and banks. However there are also less obvious influences. For example, *'signposters'*. These are people who can signpost opportunities, contacts or customers in the direction of your business.

---

## Example:

We wondered why we did not get any enquiries fed to us by a particular Enterprise Agency. The director assured us that we should be getting prospects offered. A detailed review revealed the receptionist, who referred all enquiries to consultants, did not have us on her list. It was a simple clerical error – costing us a potential £100,000 in sales per year!

### – A training business

---

How effective are your signposters? – check them out.

A second set of network contacts that are less visible but very important are the Key Influencers. To understand their part in your business requires an introduction to the idea of networking.

Networking is simply developing and maintaining relationships with the people who can affect and impact directly or indirectly on your business. It gives you access to contacts, information, leads, threats and opportunities, ideas, role models and many other benefits. Think of it like a spider's web:

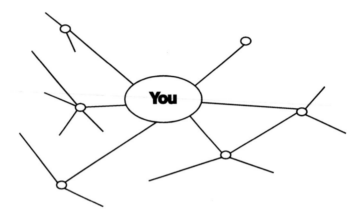

The spider's web consists of you at the centre and your key contacts. These contacts are also connected into others. By cultivating certain contacts you can have access to many of the elements that affect your business. The Key Influencers are those people at the intersections of the spider's web, the people you contact if you want to know what is really happening in one area.

*Ace Conveyors* contacted one person at British Coal to find out what was happening in the coal business in Yorkshire. The point about the key influencers is that they require nurturing and attention. Who are the key influences on your network and are they active on your behalf?

Everybody has a network. Your job is to energise it. This means building relationships and being active with the key players. Two factors clearly emerged from our research. First, top management talks regularly to their network contacts. They had their home telephone numbers and contacted them on a daily or weekly basis. Networkers had immediate access to top management at all times – and they used it.

Secondly, key players travel. Typically our successful managers are travelling 40,000 miles annually visiting customers, suppliers and their network contacts.

*"We make the foods on Monday and we are on the road Tuesday, Wednesday, Thursday, Friday networking."*
**– Derwent Valley Foods.**

Networking involves regular contact with a purpose. This can be exchanging useful information, passing on news, and doing favours. One company described the process as, "Think of how you treat your best friends and do the same with your network."

One caution – some established networks might not be appropriate for your business. One company related a tale where the chairman spent all his time 'networking' at Round Table, Chamber of Commerce lunches, The Lions and Institute of Directors dinners. He got fat but the business didn't. He got it wrong simply because none of the people who attended these functions were really part of his network (that is, they could directly influence his business).

Focus on networks that contribute towards your vision. These may not be the ones you necessarily enjoy most.

A final issue from my own business experience. Sometimes we build a strong relationship with one person as a key customer, who provides us with lots of opportunities. Then they leave and everything stops. The need is to build a network *inside* the customer's organisation so that we are not dependent on one person. Yes, I know it's obvious but we fell for it and so will you.

Are you dependent on one good relationship in a key customer?

---

## Example:

"We contacted the Northern Development Corporation to find out which companies are entering our area and we make contact with them. We go in at the highest possible level as we did with a Japanese company recently. We were in dialogue with them long before they moved here. When they did set up they knew us well..."

*– Panda Supplies*

---

## ...ASSESSMENT

## 2.2 Networking

**Tick here if this is true**
**for your business**

1. *We understand our network and how it impacts upon our business.* ❑

2. *Networking is a top management responsibility in our business.* ❑

3. *Top management spends enough time networking with key customers.* ❑

4. *We are not dependent on individual contact with key customers, we have many contacts.* ❑

5. *Networking creates more new opportunities than we can cope with.* ❑

6. *Networking is planned for at management meetings.* ❑

Less than four ticks and you need to take **ACTION...**

**...ACTION**

## 2.2 Networking

*Action 33*   Manage your network.

> <u>*Step 1*</u>: *List your key network contacts by constructing a diagram as follows:*

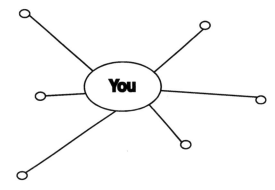

> <u>*Step 2*</u>: *Mark the names as follows:*
>
> + *if they act positively for your business*
> − *if they have a negative impact on your business*
> = *if they are neutral*

> <u>*Step 3*</u>: *Make a plan to use the + to build your business. How can you convert the − to +? How will you encourage the = to get off the fence and act positively?*
>
> *Tick those names you consider you contact frequently enough and use an X to indicate those you need to contact more frequently. Transfer these decisions into your diary or time planner.*

**Action 34**   Use your existing network to build upon who else could be of assistance to your business. Use their network to build up yours. (80% of new business in 1990 came from this ACTION alone. It works. Do it.)

**Action 35**   Start a network file. Snippets of information that might be of interest to them can be collected and passed over. Networks require energising, give as well as take. What have you done for your network this month?

It's not "Gi's a job!"... Examples of information could be:

- *Newspaper articles of interest*
- *Names in the news*
- *Books*
- *Articles*
- *A helpful contact, i.e. a name*
- *Changes in legislation, e.g. grants available*
- *An example of good practice to learn from*
- *A good idea*

What can you put in to your networks?

## ...AWARENESS

# 2.3 Problem-seeking/problem-solving

There are clearly many ways to grow and develop a business. One way is to take on the market leader or established competitor. If you do it head-on, unless you have competitive advantage recognised by customers, then you will need resources in the ratio of 3:1 to have a chance of winning business from the established competitor. For instance, if your competitor has three salesmen then you will need nine or if they spend £10,000 on advertising, you will need to spend £30,000.

The lesson is do not take on market leaders head-on (unless you have a strong competitive advantage). Our successful companies have found an alternative, they search for a gap and work through it.

This is how they do it. They spend lots of time with customers (networking). They focus on what they are good at (core skills) and they listen to customers and their problems. A customer problem becomes their opportunity.

Alternatively they go round the back; i.e.,'mugging'

They break with convention and do something completely different.

They solve the problem quickly – often jointly with the customer. If it is a new customer the process then can become problem-seeking/ problem-solving – friend for life. Let us examine the process a little more closely.

## Problems are where the business is suffering

In the summer of 1991, our customers were suffering in the recession. Their main concerns were lack of orders. There was no point trying to sell them production training, but they did need to know 'How to Create New Business'. Sometimes customers have great difficulty in articulating their problems, they may not even be aware of the true cause. Here is an opportunity for you. You can help them identify and focus on real problems – these are your opportunities.

One blockage to the process is where you go in selling; i.e., 'Here is the solution now what is your problem?'... To make this process work you need to ask questions and listen. Go over the top with the solution, make it memorable.

---

### Example:

One company identified from a customer that they were fed up with suppliers taking forever to get back to them with proposals and quotations. They returned to their office, wrote the proposal, focused the typing resources on it and returned the proposal personally the same day to the customer. Naturally they won the contract and the customer still talks to this day about it as an excellent example of customer service.

---

In summary the process looks like this:

1. *Network with customers.*
2. *Ask problem raising questions.*
3. *Identify where the pain exists.*
4. *Fix it quickly.*
5. *Exaggerate to make it memorable.*
6. *Maintain the relationship.*

---

### Example:

"Every time a representative visits a customer they have a form to complete which identifies customers' problems. This is circulated to interested parties in our business so if it's mechanical it goes to the Mechanical Engineers or electrical to the Electrical Department. We have a weekly problem-solving meeting where we review our top ten customer problems. It's called the Top Ten Committee. We then prioritise and aim to fix them fast. This has created mega-opportunities for us over the past year or so.

*– Bonas*

---

### Example:

"In 1985 the whole of the retail trade was looking at straight-on display trays. This was an innovation from Marks and Spencer. Sainsbury had a different shelf problem to Tesco. So we went to talk with them and solved a problem for each customer and we ended up with a different configuration of trays. Now that caused us a problem but it was typical of how we were first in, flexible to their needs. Everybody followed, but Derwent Valley Foods were first."

*– Derwent Valley Foods*

---

Sometimes customers will not admit to having problems but most will recognise the need to make improvements. What improvements would you like to see in your business?

The skill is to ask the right questions. These need to be problem raising questions:

- *If you could improve one thing in your business what would it be?*
- *What keeps you awake at night?*
- *What is stopping you moving forward?*

I suggest you start with the pain, even if it's not business related. One consultant gets business by helping senior managers' children with their career choices because this is a concern for them.

Once the problem is identified then the magic is created for customers by responding it at record speed. It alleviates the pain, they feel good and sleep easier in their beds.

**Problem-Seeking → Problem-Solving = Friend for Life**

# ...ASSESSMENT

## 2.3 Problem-seeking/problem-solving

**Tick here if this is true
for your business**

1. *We are good at listening to our customers rather than selling products.* ❏

2. *We use problem-seeking/problem-solving as a major source of business generation.* ❏

3. *We help our customers identify real problems* ❏

4. *We often surprise our customers with the speed and effectiveness of our problem-solving on their behalf.* ❏

5. *Our business is flexible enough to respond immediately to major opportunities.* ❏

6. *We have well proven methods for problem-seeking.* ❏

Less than 4 ticks and you need to take **ACTION...**

## ...ACTION

## 2.3   Problem-seeking/problem-solving

**Action 36**   Read Toolkit 2. An introduction to the process of problem-seeking/problem-solving. This is the heart of Hallmarks. Circulate it to your customer contact people. Tell them this is how we now do business around here.

**Action 37**   Here is how to use the problem-seeking/problem-solving process to create major sales opportunities:

> <u>Step 1:</u> *Arrange a meeting with a new/existing customer. Once you have established that you are dealing with a decision maker, say: "To enable me to really understand your business and how we can best support you, do you mind if I ask you a few questions?" Clearly this process can only be used with the key decision makers in the buying process. If you find that you are meeting a purchasing clerk, not the decision maker, then the way to identify the key people in the buying process without insulting the purchasing clerk is to ask this question: "If we were to become a supplier to your company what would be the process that we would need to go through to achieve buyer status?" This question will help you identify the right people to meet.*

> <u>Step 2:</u> *Ask the following questions to seek to identify problems. Use those that suit your style or invent your own.*
> - *What improvements would you like to see in your business?*

86

- *What is causing you difficulty right now?*
- *What one thing would help you sleep easy in your bed?*
- *What would have the biggest impact on your business?*
- *Where could you get the biggest bang for your buck?*
- *What blockages face you?*
- *What's stopping you achieving your goals?*

*Make up your own problem-seeking questions.*

<u>Step 3</u>: *Once the customer has identified an issue, help them examine it in detail with the following probing questions.*

- *What effect is that (problem) having?*
- *What does your boss think about it?*
- *What will the long-term effect be?*
- *What will be the knock-on effect to your customers?*

*Again, invent your own problem probing questions.*

<u>Step 4</u>: *Ask: "If we could help you resolve that (problem) would you be happy?"*

<u>Step 5</u>: *Where possible fix the problem at lightning speed to create customer delight.*

<u>Step 6</u>: *Develop your relationship and seek more business.*

**Action 38**   Find a theme that is common for customers and go seeking the issue. For instance, every training organisation has problems with evaluation of timing. So I would ask what problem do you have with evaluation? (Knowing they are bound to have problems).

Problems likely to concern customers are:.

1. ..................................................................

2. ..................................................................

3. ..................................................................

4. ..................................................................

5. ..................................................................

6. ..................................................................

**Action 39**    Develop your own list of problem-seeking questions. Train your people to ask them.

Q1. ..............................................................

Q2. ..............................................................

Q3. ..............................................................

Q4. ..............................................................

Q5. ..............................................................

Q6. ..............................................................

**Action 40**    Practise asking questions and listening for clues. Practise staying quiet whilst customers pour out their concerns. It's hard work but watch the business flow in!

**Action 41**    Fix some problems at express speed. Do something in one hour that normally takes you a week. Watch the customer's eyes light up!

List things that would amaze your customers.

1. ..................................................................

2. ..................................................................

3. ..................................................................

4. ..................................................................

5. ..................................................................

6. ..................................................................

**Action 42**    Share success and ideas with colleagues so they too can delight your customers.

**...AWARENESS**

## 2.4 Customer delight

*– Surprising customers with the level of service you provide*

Customer delight is normally personal, customer service is corporate. You know if you are delighting customers by the amount of unsolicited new business they offer you. This is the acid test. Customer service will maintain your customer base and order level, delight by definition extends it. If customers are really delighted they normally act on it rather than simply say thank you.

---

### *Example:*

"It's not enough simply to satisfy your customers in today's business world. You have to delight them. You do this by addressing a whole number of areas, personal integrity, quality delivery and giving that little bit extra."

*– Bonas*

---

Customer delight is tough but worth it. It is also different to customer service. Both are needed. Customer service is a right!

Time for some more examples:

## *Example:–*

A friend ordered some new carpets for a new house. The day they moved in he opened the door to be met by a mountain of offcuts in the hall. After moving that, he found all the doors had been taken off so he had to store them in the garage. 2 hours later he was able to move in his furniture.

Having had that experience, next time he moved he sought another carpet fitter. This time he opened the door to find not a thread anywhere (Customer Service). The doors had been refitted and opened properly. (Customer Service). But the best bit was yet to come. In the kitchen was a small vase with some freesias and a card which read "Mrs Jones, welcome to your new home." – The Carpet Fitter (Customer Delight). A light-hearted example yet that guy could have as much business as he liked, the ladies loved him. They told everybody all —the time. He did not need to advertise.

## *Example:*

A customer lived in Scotland but supported Blackpool Football Club. In 1991 Blackpool reached the semi-final of a Cup. This guy in Scotland was desperate for a ticket but could not get one. The supplier on hearing of this dispatched a secretary from Sheffield to Blackpool to obtain tickets for the match. They sent them by courier to their customer the same day. (OK a bit more than customer service at this point). But the best was yet to come. At half time the customer was welcomed over the tannoy by name and asked to report to the director's suite after the match. Awaiting him and his colleague was a bottle of champagne courtesy of the company, together with a signed photograph of his favourite team as a reminder of the day.

The ingredients in customer delight:

* *Satisfaction beyond the norm*
* *Spontaneous or unexpected*
* *Often a personal touch*
* *Speed*
* *Attention to detail*

The results of customer delight often are:

* *It makes people feel good*
* *They tell everybody about it*
* *It leads to more business being offered*
* *It is offered without the expectation of reciprocation; i.e., it is not emotional blackmail, it is genuine.*

The challenge is to delight not embarrass customers.

---

### *Example:*

One successful company decided not to attend the industry exhibition at the National Exhibition Centre but to take their customers on the Orient Express. It was a memorable day, which everyone enjoyed. The customers spent the next twelve months asking what was happening next? Most importantly, sales increased from these customers by 16% in the year – well above expectations.

---

Customer delight can set new standards and create expectations, which are hard to follow. But it's fantastic when it works!!

It's not enough in today's business to satisfy the customer, what you have to do is delight them.

## *Example:-*

Imagine putting your dog into kennels when you go on holiday. They look after your dog excellently. It looks healthy and happy with bright eyes, a wet nose and a shining coat on your return. (Customer satisfaction to this point).

Back at the house however there is a postcard from your dog who also claims to have been on holiday! (Customer delight). You see, you are smiling at the prospect. Also – at Christmas you get a card from your dog wishing you a Happy Christmas.

**– Triple A Animal Hotel & Care Centre**

# ...ASSESSMENT

## 2.4  Customer Delight

**Tick here if this is true**
**for your business**

1. *We have customer friendly front line people.* ☐

2. *We create a high level of unsolicited repeat business by delighting our customers.* ☐

3. *Customers often express surprise at the speed of our response.* ☐

4. *We can provide six good examples of customer delight from our last months business.* ☐

5. *Customers' complaints are often turned into delight by the speed and quality of our response.* ☐

6. *I have experienced customer delight.* ☐

Less than 4 ticks and you need to take **ACTION**...

# ...ACTION

## 2.4   Customer Delight

You may recall how we defined customer delight:

• *Customer satisfaction is satisfaction with the performance of a product or service.*
• *Customer delight adds personal satisfaction building the self-esteem of the customer. How the customer feels about it at a personal level.*

Here are some actions to take: Note, these are examples only. By definition customer delight is created by personal actions.

*Action 43*   Send a personal note thanking someone.

*Action 44*   A bottle of champagne when someone is promoted.

*Action 45*   Customer's name on a spot in your car park. (Rather than the directors'!)

*Action 46*   Customer's name on teacup when they visit you.

*Action 47*   Your staff sends customer a signed birthday card.

*Action 48*   You invite your customer and wife (or husband) out to dinner to celebrate their wedding anniversary.

*Action 49*   A card sent from holiday.

**Action 50**   Here is a way to link customer delight into your normal customer service activities.

*Step 1:* Get a team of your people together (4-5) these do not have to be the top team. Get a flip chart and pen or drawing board.

*Step 2:* Draw your normal order/delivery cycle – from receiving an enquiry to receiving payment. It might look like this:

| Telephone Enquiry | Sales Visit | Quote | Order Placed | Confirmed | Goods Despatched | After Sales | Payment Received |

*Step 3:* Brainstorm – where in this cycle can we create customer delight by surprising ourcustomer? Where would we have most impact?

*Step 4:* Take action.

# ...AWARENESS

# 2.5 Market development

## – The route to successful business growth

Successful companies create a recipe based on their experiences of solving customer problems and use it. They aim to apply this as widely as possible.

'Sticking to the knitting' and focusing on core skills is the way our successful companies developed.

Clearly additional skills can be developed over time but our companies do not appear to get involved in developing totally new products or services. They ask the questions: Are we making the most of the products and services we already possess? Who else can we sell them to?

The product and service evolves over time and is slowly shaped by changing customer needs.

Sometimes companies diversify away from their existing products because of boredom. One engineering company in Consett considered (after the MD had a holiday in Florida) opening a hamburger bar in Newcastle. They forgot that McDonalds have a few years more experience at it. They eventually decided to stick to engineering because the hamburger bar was not part of their core strategy. They had a good product, which they sold in the North East. They now sell it all over the UK and make lots of money.

The way successful companies create more customers is through the establishment of an effective Business Generation System (B.G.S.).

The purpose of the B.G.S. is to create opportunities to sell and develop new business.

It could be that for one business the B.G.S. is mailout and telephone follow-up. This might create all the new business. In other businesses it could be attending trade exhibitions. In my business it is presenting papers to conferences. The B.G.S. ensures we get to sufficient conferences to present enough papers to build our business.

The real issues with B.G.S. is that the channel of communication with your market will be different in every case. Two key questions to ask are:

1. *Where do I get my new business from?*
2. *Have I a system that generates enough new opportunities to meet the business objectives.*

Interestingly over 90% of our clients consult us for marketing when they really mean a system to create new business. In the section on ACTION I show you how to set about creating enough opportunities to satisfy your business needs.

---

### Example:–

*AbleClean* of Hartlepool wrote to one of my people recently thanking him because the business generating system had increased sales in the first six months by 41%. They originally requested a marketing plan and an idea for diversification.

---

# DIVERSIFICATION AND COMPLETE NEW PRODUCT IDEAS

## LOG SHEET

Please write all your new ideas here for diversification and complete new products (where you have little knowledge or expectation).

1. ........................................................................................................
2. ........................................................................................................
3. ........................................................................................................
4. ........................................................................................................
5. ........................................................................................................
6. ........................................................................................................
7. ........................................................................................................
8. ........................................................................................................
9. ........................................................................................................
10. ........................................................................................................
11. ........................................................................................................
12. ........................................................................................................

When you get to the bottom of this page please tear out carefully and burn!

# ...ASSESSMENT

## 2.5   Market Development

**Tick here if this is true
for your business**

1.  *We grow by selling our proven products/services
    to more customers.*  ❏

2.  *We do not expend major resources on diversification
    (unless there is no other option).*  ❏

3.  *We plan for and allocate sufficient resources to
    develop new markets.*  ❏

4.  *We only get involved in bringing new products to
    market when there is a significant demand.*  ❏

5.  *Long term prospects in our primary markets are
    excellent.*  ❏

6.  *We have an effective business generating system to
    create new business.*  ❏

Less than four ticks and you need to take **ACTION...**

**...ACTION**

## 2.5   Market Development

Market development is not only undertaken when existing markets are either saturated or under threat; it should happen constantly.

**Action 51**   Assess the opportunities for greater market share. How big are they? What is your share? What does the future look like? What threats (if any) exist?

**Action 52**   Identify the next natural step for your business. Successful companies develop their markets concentrating often geographically.

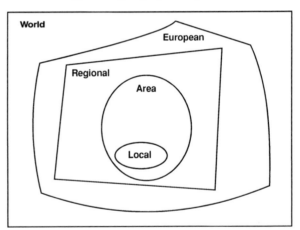

What is your next natural market extension?

**Action 53**   Create a resource (person) to develop a network for your next step. Find out who supplies? What is the potential? Who are the key contacts?

Remember, the skills required to build a new network are different from those of maintaining an existing network.

**Action 54**  Develop an effective Business Generating System using the process that follows:

**Buying Platform:**   Sales target x production lead time.

**Working Platform:**   Monthly sales target x conversion rate of enquiries.

**Market Platform:**   Working platform x conversion rate x 'thinking lead-time' in months.

*Step 1: Calculate target annual sales.*

*Step 2: Calculate average order size from historical records.*

*Step 3: Calculate number of orders required for year.*

$$Calculation: \quad \frac{Step\ 1}{Step\ 2} \ = \ No\ of\ orders$$

*Step 4: Decide how many orders will come from existing customers (Buying Platform).*

*Step 5: Determine how many new orders required.*

*Calculation: Step 3 – Step 4 = New orders required*

*Step 6: Calculate Conversion Rate of quotes to orders (e.g., 3 quotes to 1 order)*

*Step 7: Calculate number of new orders required.*

*Calculation: multiply Step 5 x Step 6*

*At this point divide the answer by 12. This gives new orders per month. Build in any seasonality, e.g. no orders at Xmas!*

*Step 8:* Determine conversion rate of new prospects to quotes; e.g., 4 new prospects to 1 quotation.

*Step 9:* Calculate number of prospects required.

Calculation: Multiply Step 7 x Step 8.
Divide by 12 to obtain monthly figure.

This is the arithmetic of the B.G.S.. Now you need to work out how to create the business on a regular basis. This time work from Step 9.

*Step 10:* Determine how new prospects are best created in your business, i.e. mailshots, telephone calls, adverts, exhibitions, etc.

Plan to undertake this activity monthly to create the level of prospects required at Step 9. Use worksheet provided.

# SALES PLAN WORKSHEET

A. *Determine last year's turnover*                                          --------

B. *Determine total number of orders last year*                    --------

C. *Determine how many orders came from*
   *repeat business (existing Customers)*                            --------

D. *Calculate % of repeat business (C − B) x 100*             --------

E. *Calculate average order size (A − B)*                           --------

F. *Establish next year's target turnover*                           --------

G. *Calculate total number of orders required*
   *next year (F − E)*                                                          --------

H. *Determine number of repeat business orders*
   *expected (G − D)*                                                           --------

I. *Calculate number of extra orders needed*
   *from new Customer (G − H)*                                         --------

J. *Determine how many quotations sent out*
   *last year and how many won.*                                      -- *in* --

K. *Determine how many prospects visited and*
   *how many asked you to quote*                                    -- *in* --

L. *Calculate how many extra quotations need*
   *to be sent out to new customers (I x Ratio J)*             --------

M. *Calculate how many potential new*
   *Customers need to be identified (L x Ratio K)*           --------

*103*

3.1
Structure/
Roles

3.5
Support
network
partnerships

3.2
Customer
partnerships

**HALLMARK 3:
Partnering**

3.4
Supplier
partnerships

3.3
Staff
partnerships

# Hallmark 3 – Partnering

## OVERVIEW

Creating and maintaining partnerships with everyone who affects your business is a Hallmark of successful companies. This chapter shows you how to develop profitable partnerships.

*Hallmark 3:* *Partnering* outlines the key principles involved in the process.

This process is defined as working in partnership with people who affect your business.

Working in partnership involves harnessing the creative talents and energies of everyone who can affect your business. The effect is that everyone, from staff through to suppliers and customers, works together for mutual gain. This process adds real value by avoiding adverse relationships and recognising that success comes from long-term commitments and not short-term 'deals'. This Section shows you how to partner successfully.

**...AWARENESS**

# 3.1 Structure/Roles

### – *Adding value to the organisation it serves*

Your organisation structure should be designed to support your business plan. This is of crucial importance. If you are extending your markets does your organisation's structure support this aim? Have staff enough time to focus on the opportunities? One company planned to go into Europe. The owner told me he would get to it when he had time among his other priorities! (Rate their chances of making it happen quickly and effectively on a scale of 1-10...)

You obviously have choices about how you organise. Without exception, our successful companies structure their business to support their business plans and, most importantly, to keep people close to customers. A priority is to stay close to customers themselves.

One problem that growth and success can bring is how you structure your business. The temptation is to add more levels as you employ more people. Therefore as you grow you can move away from the customers. The entrepreneur becomes an administrator. This is so important it is worthy of elaboration.

The diagram overleaf illustrates the changing structural interface between entrepreneur and customer as the business grows.

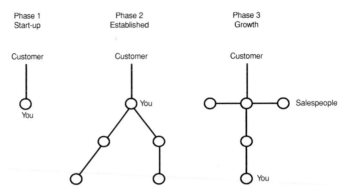

At Phase 1 business stays close to the customer because there are few choices! You know the customer personally because you are dealing with them all the time. At Phase 2 as you grow in size and take on more people, you have choices. You can maintain your customer contacts or delegate them.

If customers have a relationship with you which is the primary reason they buy, then stick with it. If they don't, then you can delegate.

At Phase 3 the choices are more difficult. As you grow, inevitably more people are contacting customers. The crucial choice is where you fit in.

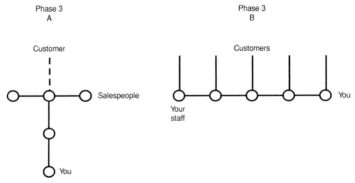

Phase 3A is the classic growth structure. The entrepreneur becomes the manager and stops seeing customers.

Phase 3B is an alternative. The entrepreneur continues his customer contacts while other people develop their own customers.

All our growth companies who were successful operate a Phase 3B structure.

How are you structured – Phase 3A or 3B?

3B allows the key players to travel and maintain customer contact. They are not deskbound running meetings and sending memos. But it is necessary to work harder at lateral information flow, to prevent overlap. Our experience shows the benefits are worth the effort.

Having thought about your structure and ensured it supports the business plan the next step is to consider what people in the structure do to build partnerships.

The concept of partnering extends beyond customers to every key contact that affects your business, both internal and external.

How do partnerships work? Here are some guidelines:

| | |
|---|---|
| **Commitment:** | *The reason the partners are working together must be important enough to get people involved. It can't be half-hearted.* |
| **Win-win:** | *The aim must be mutual benefit for both sides in the partnership. One must not be seen to be constantly gaining at the expense of the other.* |
| **Long Term View:** | *Partnerships are long-term between stable organisations. Short-term relationships are not partnerships.* |
| **Openness:** | *Both partners should keep each other informed. .. Surprises can be deadly.* |
| **Development:** | *Trust does not happen quickly. It takes time to develop.* |
| **Effective Representation:** | *Both sides need a champion to marshal resources and make things happen.* |
| **Integration:** | *Both sides need to be.* |

The key is, then, to make these principles work in practice. How can you support this process?

Do you build effective partnerships?

# ...ASSESSMENT

## 3.1 Structure/Roles

**Tick here if this is true
for your business**

1. *Our organisation structure supports our business plan.* ☐

2. *Our organisation structure ensures the right people stay as close as possible to our customers.* ☐

3. *Starting from scratch, given a clean sheet of paper we would create exactly the same structure as we have right now.* ☐

4. *We aim to build partnerships with all our key people.* ☐

5. *Our business is built on partnership principles.* ☐

6. *Partnerships are intrinsic to our business success.* ☐

Less than four ticks and you need to take **ACTION...**

# ...ACTION

## 3.1 Structure/Roles

**Action 55**   Start with a clean sheet of paper, consider your future plans. Forget your existing business. What structure would ideally serve your future plans? Draw this on a sheet of paper. Compare this to your existing situation. What does this tell you? Take action to prepare for the future. Redraw the chart. Take out levels. Get key people closer to your customers.

**Action 56**   Redraw your structure to enable you to spend at least 30% of your time with customers.

**Action 57**   Publish your structure so that people know where they fit.

**Action 58**   Get your top people together. Discuss the idea of partnering. What kinds of partnerships would make sense for us? How well do we manage our partnerships?

| *List your partnerships.* | *Tick which are effective/not effective* | |
| --- | --- | --- |
| | **+** | **-** |
| 1............................................ | ☐ | ☐ |
| 2............................................ | ☐ | ☐ |
| 3............................................ | ☐ | ☐ |
| 4............................................ | ☐ | ☐ |
| 5............................................ | ☐ | ☐ |
| 6............................................ | ☐ | ☐ |

**Action 59**   Ask your people to keep a time log for a week. See how much time is actually spent in partnerships?

# ...AWARENESS

3.2
Customer
partnerships

# 3.2 Customer Partnerships

### – Adding value to your customer's business

*"People buy people first" – Metro Radio*

A test of the quality of your customer partnerships is the level of repeat business you get. The acid test is when you mess up and let your customer down and still keep the business. It is as simple as this: the better the quality of your partnership with your customer the more business you will get from them.

The exception to this rule is where you have a really unique product that is unavailable elsewhere.

How do you develop customer partnerships? Here is the best method I know.

1. *Decide how you like to be treated as a customer.*
2. *Compare this with how you treat your best customer.*
3. *Repeat Step 1 & 2 with customers, covering 80% of your business.*

---

**Example:**

Yes, we know them (customers) very well. We build relationships; if we can't build a relationship with a customer we think hard about whether we want the business. We have very good customer relationships...

*– Cresstale*

---

Very often when we have conducted detailed Customer Perception Surveys for our clients the concerns expressed by customers are about the lack of partnership. Typical comments would be:

- *"We only hear from you when you are chasing orders – you never contact us at other times."*
- *"It is not that you delivered late, it is the fact you did not let us know."*
- *"We do not have a name to contact when we have queries."*
- *"You never return our calls promptly."*
- *"You seem to operate in the belief that: 'It would be a good business if it was not for our customers.'"*
- *"We never feel confident that we can trust you."*

If we treated our best friends in similar ways, would they stay around for long? It seems to me that the real meanings behind these very common complaints are:

- *You don't communicate with us*
- *You do not treat us with any respect*
- *There is no relationship, we are just a sale to you*
- *You do nothing to build our self-esteem in fact, quite the opposite.*

People like people who are like themselves

Rapport can be established if you become like the person that you are dealing with. If you mirror customer behaviour they like you, build rapport and you will build sales. Listen to how they talk, they will either say 'I like what I see' (visual). Tell me the benefits (auditory) or it feels OK (emotional). Talk back to them in the same way (visual, audibly or emotional) and watch sales develop.

This technique is called Neuro Linguistic Programming (NLP) just in case you want to impress your friends in the pub!

---

### *Example:*

A company was surprised when a competitor came along and offered their customer of five years' standing the same product at a few pounds less and took away their business. The chairman told me he was shocked and felt let down. I asked about the quality of the partnership with the customer. He told me he thought it was OK because they had few written complaints over the years....

---

The principle is that people like people who are like themselves, and if we communicate in their way they will like us and buy from us. If we get the message confused they may not; e.g., if they are visual and you talk (auditory/at them for hours) guess what will happen..... Practise the technique or better still read up the method in more detail (see ACTIONS).

---

## WHY CUSTOMERS QUIT!

1% Die

3% Move away

5% Develop Other Friendships

9% For Competitive Reasons

14% Because of Product Dissatisfaction

## 68% Quit because of
## ATTITUDE OF INDIFFERENCE
## TOWARDS CUSTOMER BY SUPPLIER!

---

There is a difference between relationships and partnerships which can be represented as follows:

## Level 1: Customer Relationships

The starting point is to treat customers like friends. One salesman in our research suggested. "My objective on any first call is to get an invite back." This seems a good starting point. His second objective was: "To understand my customers' business better than they do." Again a superb objective. The first starts a relationship, the second consolidates it. Beyond that, follow the maxim, treat my customers like my best friends.

The benefit will be a long-term business relationship.

## Level 2: Partnerships

Building partnerships with customers goes beyond simple courtesies of communication and treating them with respect. It requires you to find ways of adding value to your customers' business for them. My salesman friend again had a view on this: "I build real partnerships by helping my customers add value to their business. I need to understand the needs of my customer's customers".

One small independent brewery gets its sales team to help publicans with their merchandising. This helps the publican to sell more products and make more money. Most of their competitors simply take orders. Guess who gets the business...

How can you add value to your customers' business?

The ideal partnership is synergistic. You are able to contribute to a degree that helps them improve their business – hence they buy even more from you..

This result is long-term commitment.

Research has established that it costs as much as 3 times the amount to create a new customer as to keep an existing one.

Creating partnerships is not simply altruistic, it is sound commercial sense.

The successful business needs to start by establishing relationships and build on these to create successful partnerships. The process can be summarised as follows:

**Start a Relationship**    -    *Aim to be invited back.*

**Maintain a Relationship**   -    *Understand your customers' business better than they do*

**Create a Partnership**    -    *Understand your customers' customer in order to help them add real value to their business.*

# ...ASSESSMENT

## 3.2   Customer Partnerships

**Tick here if this is true
for your business**

1. *The quality of our customer partnerships is a major business strength.* ❏

2. *We enjoy a high level of repeat business and referrals.* ❏

3. *Some of our key customer's are our best friends.* ❏

4. *We aim to understand our customer's business better than they do.* ❏

5. *We add real value to our customers business by working in partnership.* ❏

6. *We build partnerships by trying to understand our customer's customer.* ❏

Less than 4 ticks and you need to take **ACTION...**

# ...ACTION

## 3.2   Customer Partnerships

***Action 60***    Give your home telephone to your key customers.

***Action 61***    Find out your key customer's main interest. Take them to an event, give them tickets, do something exciting for them.

***Action 62***    Ring your key customers daily/weekly/monthly (whichever is appropriate) regardless of the level of business.

***Action 63***    Take your key customers out for a beer – find out about them: interests, hobbies, ambitions, hopes, fears. Build a friendship. Your aim is not to talk shop.

***Action 64***    Give out some free samples. You may take your product for granted, your customer won't.

***Action 65***    Think further about building partnerships with your customers. Are they hurting? What can you do to help? How can you help them add value to their business?

| *Key Customers* | *Current Problems* | *Where we can help* |
| --- | --- | --- |
| 1. ............ | | |
| 2. ............ | | |
| 3. ............ | | |
| 4. ............ | | |

5. .................................................................
6. .................................................................
7. .................................................................
8. .................................................................
9. .................................................................
10. ...............................................................
11. ...............................................................
12. ...............................................................
13. ...............................................................
14. ...............................................................
15. ...............................................................

**Action 66**   Agree to talk to some of your customer's customers. Make a list of their needs. Talk to your customer about how you can help to help them.

**Action 67**   Mirror your customer's behaviour in front of them. This creates rapport. People are either:

- **Visual** (Show me)
- **Auditory** (Tell me), or
- **Feeling** (Convince me [emotions])

*Step 1:* List your key customers.

*Step 2:* At your next meetings observe and try to respond on each level:

- *Visual*
- *Auditory*
- *Emotional*

...*by listening carefully to how they talk.*

*Step 3:* Talk to them from the same position:

- *Visual (Show them)*
- *Auditory (Tell them)*
- *Emotional (Convince them emotionally)*

**Action 68**   Read more about NLP. See: *Influencing with Integrity* by Genie Z. Laborde (Syntony Publishing, CA 1983), or *Your Ticket to Success* by Alex Mcmillan (Management Books 2000, 1997)

## ...AWARENESS

3.3
Staff
partnerships

# 3.3   Staff Partnerships

## *– Creating Mutually Beneficial Contracts*

---

### *Example:*

**I once had a boss who could get me to walk through brick walls for him. I had another who could not motivate me to get out of bed in the morning.**

Boss 1:

The annual appraisal. Picture the situation. I was invited into the boss's office. He instructed his secretary to hold all calls and make us two coffees. We sat around a low coffee table, jackets off, ties loosened. He informed me that he had been giving considerable thought to my job and me. He appeared to have made copious notes. He told me how much he appreciated my work. I noticed he had put one of my reports up to the Chairman with my name still on it and an attached note "David has done a superb job on this project". He told me he had investigated some development opportunities and had talked to a business school, and gave me a prospectus for an M.B.A. He had cleared it with the chairman, got the funds and paved the way. He finished the appraisal like this: "David, it's Ellen's birthday on Saturday (my partner). Take her out to dinner on us". He was

---

like this all the time... If he rang me tomorrow (I haven't seen him in twenty years) and asked me to go to London at six am the following day, my answer (twenty years on) would be: "Tony, do you want me to run with a sack of coal on my back via Glasgow...?"

Boss 2:

I also learnt a few lessons from my next boss. He used to call me Richard... All my reports to the Chairman had my name Tippexed out and replaced by his own. Two days before the annual appraisal (which I looked forward to – I quite enjoyed discussing my future), he cancelled. "Important meeting with the Chairman, Richard...." I learnt later he was playing golf! Three weeks later he instructed me to fill in the appraisal myself, saying he would "sign it sometime..."

Most managers are familiar with the theory of getting the best from people and building staff relationships. Like many aspects of management, putting the theory into practice is the key problem. It is a particular challenge for fast-growth businesses, however, because customer delight is created by effective employees – internal customers. How you treat your people will directly impact on your customers. How effective are your human assets?

There are many books on motivation. I personally have a problem with the concept. Fifty years of research into motivation has failed to produce motivated people. Perhaps we cannot motivate others. Maybe we can only provide incentives. My incentive from Tony was the promise of the MBA. If I performed well I also got to take my partner out to dinner at the Company's expense. What incentives do you offer your people?

> ## *Example:–*
>
> One of the research companies rewarded a junior clerk for exceptional performance by buying her and her friend two tickets to see 'New Kids on the Block'. They arranged transport to and from the concert and even checked with her mother that she did not mind her daughter being kept out late. A memorable night for the young lady that stayed in her mind far longer than any cash bonus.

Would your people do anything for you or do they disappear like lightning at 5 o'clock? Building staff partnerships requires attention to a simple model:

1. *Recruit the right people – look beyond and behind the c.v.*
2. *Give them clear objectives.*
3. *Train them continuously.*
4. *Review their performance. Communicate continually, providing feedback.*
5. *Reward good and punish poor performance.*

These five steps will enable you to build a partnership with your people and provide good performance for your business. This is management.

There are many ways of enhancing employee partnerships. Here are some examples.

- *Providing business cards for everyone, including the juniors.*
- *Pictures of staff in reception.*
- *A Christmas bonus in which highest paid receive the same as the lowest.*
- *Same job titles for everyone – Partner.*

---

## Example:–

*Keepmoat* set out to raise £50,000 during 1991 for the blind appeal. They asked the staff to organise 'It's a Knockout!' over a weekend. People worked 24 hours a day. The appeal raised over £70,000, involved everybody in the business and wasa tremendous team-building success. Incidentally, the MD had himself put in the stocks to have wet sponges thrown at him by employees...Now, that is the meaning of 'building relationships'!

---

## Letting Go

Undoing a key blockage in growing a business is for the owner to let go and share power with their team.

When a business starts, the entrepreneur often does everything, driving the business with energy and inspiring their people. However the business gets to a point where the entrepreneur cannot possibly do everything. Their strength (individual control) becomes the business' weakness. They need to learn to delegate and let go.

Most business books talk about delegation as if it were a simple process. However it is actually very difficult for entrepreneurs to share power, delegate and let go.

Our successful businesses let go of the rope gradually until they build confidence in the performance of their people. Letting go is a psychological, not a business management issue.

It becomes a business management issue however when the need to control becomes obsessive, resulting in continual interference and overriding of key management decisions, sudden changes of direction and a company atmosphere that is dictated by the mood the boss is in this morning...

Responsibility without authority is not delegation.

# ...ASSESSMENT

## 3.3 Staff Partnerships

**Tick here if this is true
for your business**

1. *Our people give 110%* ☐

2. *Our people provide us with a competitive advantage.* ☐

3. *We operate on a true partnership business with our people.* ☐

4. *We have a clear set of incentives for our staff which encourage that bit extra commitment.* ☐

5. *Our people take responsibility and produce results beyond our expectations.* ☐

6. *I have been able to 'let go' in order to develop our business.* ☐

Less than four ticks and you need to take **ACTION...**

## ...ACTION

## 3.3  Staff Partnerships

***Action 69***    Analyse your human assets as a prelim developing partnerships.

*Step 1: Place each of your key people in the framework below.*
*Note: This framework considers value to the business without demeaning people.*

|  | | LOW | HIGH |
|---|---|---|---|
| **PRODUCTIVITY** | HIGH | PEAKED PERFORMER | STARS |
|  | LOW | MISMATCH | PROBLEM PERFORMER |
|  | | LOW | HIGH |

**UNUSED POTENTIAL**

*Step 2: Key Questions:*

- *If you found this difficult to do, how well do you know your people?*

- *Actions build partnerships with your stars and your peaked performers. Sort out your problem performers and deal with any mismatches.*

**Action 70**    Test your people management system against our
five step model. How effective is your system of
staff management?

**Action 71**    Introduce some new incentives for your people, find
out what turns them on and then provide it.

**Action 72**    Ask your people to review your performance. Start
the process of leadership today!

| *What do I do well?* | *What do I do badly?* |
|---|---|
| *1..* | *1.* |
| *2.* | *2.* |
| *3.* | *3.* |
| *4.* | *4.* |
| *5.* | *5.* |
| *6.* | *6.* |

| *What should I improve?* | *What training should I undertake?* |
|---|---|
| *1.* | *1.* |
| *2.* | *2.* |
| *3.* | *3.* |
| *4.* | *4.* |
| *5.* | *5.* |
| *6.* | *6.* |

**Action 73**    Do something memorable for your people, i.e.:

- *Give them all business cards.*
- *Take them out to dinner.*
- *Listen to them.*
- *Take them with you on joint visits.*
- *Tell them about your high level meetings and
dealings.*

**Action 74**  When you need to let go try this process:

- *Pick the right people to delegate to.*
- *Agree an objective or a task.*
- *Ask them to prepare a one-page bullet point plan how they might achieve it.*
- *Review the plan before action is taken. Provide any coaching or help.*
- *Let them get on with it.*
- *Show interest.*
- *Celebrate success or lessons.*

This gradual letting-go process works and reduces the stress of sharing power by doing it in a gradual, controlled manner.

3.4
Supplier
partnerships

# ...AWARENESS

# 3.4 Supplier Partnerships

## *– Ensuring supplies*

---

### *Example:–*

"We also visited and made presentations to our key suppliers because suppliers are a major element of our financial resources. We tell them about our plans, how our sales are going, keep them informed about what we are trying to do. We made commitments to them about payment, so when we said we wanted a delivery, there was one. They were more willing to help us develop our business and getting credit was no problem. They helped us over the humps and bumps."

**– Derwent Valley Foods**

---

### *Example:–*

"We have a lot of specialist arrangements with suppliers. We go for single sourcing whenever we can. We enter three-year agreements with them. This enables us to control cost quality and operate tight delivery schedules. We work in partnership to the benefit of both parties"

**– Bonas**

---

Successful companies treat their suppliers as an integral part of their business. It is difficult to see any difference between the way they treat customers, staff or suppliers.

They all have similar characteristics:

- *Long-term view*
- *Two-way benefits*
- *Win/win relationships*
- *Mutual respect and trust*
- *High performance standard*
- *Ongoing communications*
- *Reduction of 'surprises' on both sides*

Clearly, just as these companies problem solve for their customers, suppliers are encouraged to do the same for them.

*Neat Ideas* management undertook a strategic training programme. They encouraged a major supplier to undertake the same training to ensure he supplied them adequately.

Successful companies build 'teams' of staff, customers and suppliers working together. They do not operate in isolation, letting customers down and kicking suppliers

How do you build partnerships with your supplier? Clearly, supplier partnerships ensure continuous supplies.

One company sends cheques with orders. Crazy? Until you realise that the supplier stockholds and the company gets a 3-hour delivery service, *Guaranteed!* Guess who gets the best service when the supplier is really pushed...? In addition, the supplier provides many new product opportunities and ideas. "They are almost part of our own business..."

Whilst switching to a cash-with-order system or pay-on-invoice might cause short term liquidity problems for your business, in the long run it will balance out. You need no longer be managing cash flow at your suppliers' expense, with the risk of incurring unmanageable debt.

# ...ASSESSMENT

## 3.4 Supplier Partnerships

**Tick here if this is true
for your business**

1. *We have long-term contracts with our suppliers.* ❑

2. *We communicate our plans and requirements to our suppliers continuously.* ❑

3. *We treat our suppliers like we treat our customers.* ❑

4. *Our suppliers are an integral part of our business to the extent that they support our competitive thrust.* ❑

5. *We encourage our suppliers to develop in line with our plans.* ❑

6. *Our suppliers supply us with ideas and innovation which helps us develop our business* ❑

Less than four ticks and you need to take **ACTION...**

## ...ACTION

# 3.4   Supplier Partnerships

*Action 75*   Carry out a supplier attitude survey. What do they think of us as customers?

*Step 1: Ask them:*

- *What do you look for in customers?*
- *Do we match up?*
- *How do we treat you as a supplier?*
- *How could we work in partnership?*
- *What could you contribute to our business?*

*Step 2: Ask your key suppliers the questions.*

*Step 3: Analyse the results:*

- *How can we create partnerships?*
- *How can we derive greater mutual benefit?*
- *What value can your suppliers add to your business in terms of:*
  - *ideas*
  - *products*
  - *solutions to problems*
  - *information*
  - *money*

*Action 76*   Consider introducing a Supplier of the Year award. Announce the winner publicly.

*Action 77*   Invite your suppliers into your business show them how their products work in your process. Ask how they could help improve your business.

**Action 78**    Communicate your plans to your key supplier. Ask for their help in developing your business.

**Action 79**    Consider entering long-term deals with key suppliers, in order to guarantee a supply of key resources.

3.5
Support
network
partnerships

# 3.5 Support Network Partnerships

## – *Ensuring your support network adds value*

Support networks are those individuals and organisations that are available to develop and assist your business, outside the direct relationships we have plainly discussed. The most obvious ones are:

- *Accountant*
- *Bank Manager*
- *Solicitor*
- *Shareholders*
- *Family*

As a general rule you will be contacting these key people fairly regularly. For example, most bank managers assume no news is bad news. Therefore you do need to be active in contacting them.

Bank managers are people too. They are often happy to be given a tour of your business, to be introduced to your team, and to be treated as an important stakeholder rather than as a necessary evil.

You should negotiate with your bank about overdraft rates, bank charges and the level of collateral required.

A friend told me he was paying 1.5% over base rate for his overdraft and we were paying 3%. I went back to the bank and in 2 seconds they reduced our rate to 2%. I asked why they hadn't reduced the rate previously and their reply was that I had not asked...! From that day I learnt about negotiating with my bank. Take the initiative and do the same.

Clearly, your family is crucial to supporting your business. Sir

John Harvey-Jones of ICI always made it for his wife and children's birthday parties. Now if the Chairman of one of the largest UK companies can make time, so can I, and so can you!

---

## *Example:*

"One of the most important aspects of our business is the support we have had from our wives and children. Otherwise we couldn't do it. We get absolutely no negative vibrations at all, in fact the opposite, nothing but encouragement."

*– Bonas*

---

There is a conundrum in running a business: if you are successful the business will become all-consuming. If you meet problems you need to work night and day to overcome them. Either way, the potential losers can be your family and friends. You need to plan to get a balance between work and home. Easy in theory – hard in practice.

Other support networks can sometimes get overlooked.

- *Business Links have funds available for training and expertise. Talk to them. (LECs in Scotland).*
- *Chambers of Commerce have expertise available as well as access to many networks. Call them.*

One of the problems about running an independent business is that it can get lonely. However, there is no need to go native. There are people with funds, expertise and networks available. Make them work for you.

# ...ASSESSMENT

## 3.5   Support Network Partnerships

**Tick here if this is true
for your business**

1. *Our support network is clearly defined and well-managed.*  ☐

2. *Our support network adds value to our business.*  ☐

3. *We make space to spend time with our families and friends.*  ☐

4. *We are aware of, and have accessed, grants and expertise available to our business.*  ☐

5. *Our bank manager gets regular information and contact from us.*  ☐

6. *We are proactive with our support network.*  ☐

Less than 4 ticks and you need to take **ACTION...**

## ...ACTION

## 3.5   Support Network Partnerships

***Action 81***   Draw a diagram of your support network relationships. Example:

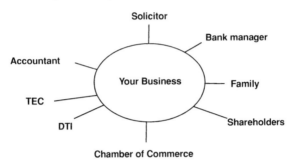

Consider your relationship with each member of your network. Do they add value to your business or have a negative impact? Mark each with +, –, or if you don't know, =.

Visit each person on your network. Talk to them about your vision for your business. What help can they provide? Find out who are on your side+, who are opposition -, or fence-sitter =.

***Action 82***   Put your partner's and children's birthdays/ anniversaries in your diary. Underline in red and work around them.

***Action 83***   Invite your bank manager to visit your operation. Treat them like customers. Introduce them to people. Agree what information you will provide monthly. Negotiate about your overdraft, bank charges and guarantee.

**Action 84**   Contact your local Business Link. Find out what training, support, advice or grants may be available.

**Action 85**   Get your accountant involved. Tell them you are tired of simply paying for audits, you want 10 good ideas, free! Tell them you are considering changing accountants!

Accountants' good ideas. (Ask them to fill this in!).

*1.* ............................................................................................

*2.* ............................................................................................

*3.* ............................................................................................

*4.* ............................................................................................

*5.* ............................................................................................

*6.* ............................................................................................

*7.* ............................................................................................

*8.* ............................................................................................

*9.* ............................................................................................

*10.* ............................................................................................

4.1
Your
personality

4.5
Changing

4.2
Business
values

**HALLMARK 4:
Personality**

4.4
Teamworking

3.3
Staff
partnerships

# Hallmark 4 – Personality

## OVERVIEW

Personality is the perceived character of the business, both internally and externally. Internally, personality creates common commitment to the vision. Externally, it provides an image to your customers. Either way, it is too important to be left to chance.

*Success companies manage their personality.*

*Hallmark 4:*     *Personality is the 'soft side' of the business which is not often discussed, particularly by hard nosed and practical business people, but which has such an impact on the effectiveness of your business that it cannot be ignored.*

Managing personality means taking actions internally so that the external face is *positive*. The challenge as businesses grow and develop is to ensure the quality of image and personality is not diluted and tarnished. Successful companies appear to be able to drive the business values into the heart of the organisation, thus ensuring that a positive external image is maintained. This Section explains how to manage personality effectively.

# ...AWARENESS

# 4.1 Your Personality

## – *Knowing yourself, to understand your business*

It has been said that the personality of the business owner and the business itself are the same. In other words, your strengths and weaknesses are mirrored in the business strengths and weaknesses. I have come to the conclusion that this is true of both large and small businesses. Can you really separate the personality of Richard Branson from Virgin, or Anita Roddick from Body Shop?

Understanding your own strengths and weaknesses can be the first step in becoming more aware of the strengths and weaknesses of your business. There are many ways of achieving this aim. You could ask your people what you are really like, or you could undertake some psychometric tests, for example:

* *OPQ5[1] (Saville Holdsworth) will tell you about your personality.*
* *Belbin[2] will tell you about your team style.*
* *Myers Briggs[3] will tell you how you relate to others, and your decision making style.*

This information can help you define your strengths and minimise your weaknesses and, as a result, those of your business.

---

1  Saville & Holdsworth Ltd, The Old Post House, 81 High St, Esher, Surrey KT10 9QA
2  Belbin Associates Ltd, The Burleigh Business Centre, 52 Burleigh St, Cambridge CB1 1DJ
3  Katherine C Briggs and Isabel Myers Briggs, Consultancy Psychology Press Inc, 577 College Avenue, Palo Alto, California 94306

Personality tests are very user-friendly these days and can be administered by technicians, i.e. consultants; they can provide very helpful insights but are not to be solely relied upon.

---

### *Example:*

A Managing Director had very poor organisational skills and her business was going nowhere. On the Belbin questionnaire, her team personality type was identified as the 'plant' (ideas person, good at shaking things up but no leadership.). Rare and valuable in a large organisation, calamitous in a small business!

She appointed a Managing Director from within who was a 'Co-ordinator/Shaper' type, while she became Chairman responsible for new products. Turnover tripled in two years as the business became co-ordinated and controlled around new market-leading ideas. She was personally enriched because she was making the best use of her strengths and seeing the business flourish.

---

The personality of the key players is influential to business success in other ways. People take their lead from you. A most important role for top management is to help the organisation develop by setting examples through their own behaviour as role models.

Not all staff are familiar with the business plan in black and white, but by observing the actions of top management people learn what is valued and expected and adjust their behaviour and priorities accordingly. This is particularly true where customer service is important: it is difficult to describe but easy to observe, experience and copy.

Symbolic actions are important for role models to consider. If top management are committed to increasing the quality of customer service at the 'sharp end' they might spend some time themselves undertaking customer service activities – rather than issuing memos.

---

### Example:

A Managing Director in our company ordered a batch of products to be publicly burnt because he found a defective item. Henceforth, everyone understood that quality mattered!

---

Clearly these actions reinforce the mission and vision. In this case the mission was to produce high quality components. The symbolic action of publicly burning the products reinforced the mission in a very powerful manner.

It is these actions and anecdotes, war stories and myths, which have a more powerful influence on people's behaviour than any business plan. The inference is clear: the key role of top management is about doing things and not just saying that things will be done.

How you spend your time is a clear signal to your business about the real business priorities.

Someone said, it is not that they don't notice (the staff) what we do, it is the fact that they do!

# ...ASSESSMENT

## 4.1   Your Personality

**Tick here if this is true
for your business**

1.  *I manage my time very effectively and act as a role
    model for our staff.*  ❏

2.  *I understand my own strengths and weaknesses and
    use this information to advantage in our business.*  ❏

3.  *I behave in line with the business priorities, sending
    the right signals to my people.*  ❏

4.  *We have many symbols that reinforce our key
    business objectives.*  ❏

5.  *I have a clear set of personal values that guide
    our decision making.*  ❏

6.  *We have undertaken psychometric tests in our
    business and use this information to build on
    strengths and minimise weaknesses.*  ❏

Less than four ticks mean you need to take **ACTION...**

# ...ACTION

## 4.1   Your Personality

**Action 85**   Undertake some psychometric tests to find out more about your personal strengths and weaknesses.
There is a contact where you can obtain information on qualified test providers:

> *The British Psychological Society*
> *St Andrews House*
> *48 Princess Road East*
> *Leicester LE1 7DR*

Adjust your role in your business to accommodate your strengths.

**Action 86**   Ask your key internal people to appraise your job performance. What do they perceive to be your strengths and weaknesses?
This is much better done 'on the run' rather than the old fashioned bureaucratic annual 'appraisal' system.

**Action 87**   Keep a time log in your diary to discover: does your use of time match your business priorities?

**Action 88**   Try some symbolic actions to reinforce the priorities of your business. If customer care is a key issue, go and contribute on the front line for a day. If a letter of thanks is received for the work of an employee, celebrate it publicly.

**Action 89**   How you spend your time
To determine the message you are giving to your people about how you value customers, estimate on

average how many hours a week you spend on the following:

*Hours*

1. *Personally with customers* -------
2. *Cutting costs* -------
3. *Visiting your own people in the field* -------
4. *Talking to other managers* -------
5. *Learning what customers think of your service* -------
6. *In meetings* -------
7. *Finding out what your customers want* -------
8. *Making technical improvement* -------
9. *Planning and scheduling* -------
10. *Recognising employees who perform well* -------

*Score*
*A = Total for odd number items (1,3,5,7,9)* --------
*B = Total for even numbered items (2,4,6,8,10)* --------

*Interpretation*
*Your total A time is that which you spend on customer care. B time is unrelated to customers. If your A time is higher the message to your people is that customers count. What kind of role model do you provide for your business?*

# ...AWARENESS

## 4.2   Business Values

### *– The set of criteria used for making decisions*

Business values are the inner aspects, the fundamental character of the business; i.e., core values and mission. Image is the external face which the business presents to the world.

Successful businesses have a clear set of business values that permeates everything they do. Many of the values have been covered in other chapters, but in summary they often include some of the following:

- *Customers come first in all our dealings.*
- *We are committed to spending the maximum amount of time with our customers.*
- *We value quality of product and customer service.*
- *We provide good products/services and can charge high prices.*
- *We personally get involved in the action, we are not desk bound.*
- *We treat all our key influences, staff, customers and suppliers with the utmost integrity.*
- *Our people are our greatest asset.*

The difference between successful companies and the rest is simply that:

Successful companies say the right words and translate them into action. Less successful ones may say the right words, but that is all.

---

### *Example:–*

Chairman's statement: *Training is important to our business...*

| | |
|---|---|
| *Employee:* | Can I do a training course? |
| *Boss:* | No. |
| *Employee:* | Then can I fund it myself and have time off? |
| *Boss:* | No. |
| *Employee:* | Why? |
| *Boss:* | Because it costs money and you might leave if we train you. |
| *Employee:* | But what about the chairman's statement: Training is important to our business? |
| *Boss:* | That's the kind of stupid thing chairmen say... |

---

Examples of core values – A Training Business:

1. *Practise what we preach.*
2. *Reward performance not status.*
3. *Quality in everything we do.*
4. *Stick to what we know.*

Values are much more than lip service. They are the core philosophy of the business. They can:

- *Define the fundamental character of the business.*
- *Create a sense of identity.*
- *Determine how resources will be allocated.*
- *Reduce confusion and game playing.*
- *Provide guidelines for implementing company plans.*

The promise on the cover of this book is "Successful Business." What is a good business? One definition, a good business:

- *Provides good financial returns to shareholders.*
- *Delights customers.*
- *Creates committed employees.*

It may also be one which has integrity in all its dealings. It has a personality that it can live with. A character it is proud of. It behaves in an ethical and moral way as well as being successful.

Somehow you know when you or your business is not behaving in line with your business values. It does not feel quite right. It causes you to think and you sense it's out of order.

---

### *Example:*

One company emphasises in all its literature that it believes in Equal Opportunities. So, how come it does not have any women in management positions?

---

### *Example:*

The MD of one small business continually talks about how important everyone is in his business. But he cannot remember the name of the receptionist.

---

# ...ASSESSMENT

## 4.2   Business Values

**Tick here if this is true
for your business**

1.  *We have a clear set of business values that guide
    our decision making.*   ❏

2.  *Our actions are consistent with our business values.*   ❏

3.  *Our values are consistently reflected by top
    management*   ❏

4.  *Everybody in our business understands our values.*   ❏

5.  *We take account of our values when we develop
    our plans.*   ❏

6.  *We have a 'good' business that behaves with integrity.*   ❏

Less than four ticks and you need to take **ACTION...**

**...ACTION**

## 4.2 Business Values

**Action 90**   Write down your core business values. Discuss them
with your key people. Are your business decisions
in line with these values? What do you need to do to
move your business back into line with your values?

*Step 1: List your core values.*

1. .................................................................
2. .................................................................
3. .................................................................
4. .................................................................
5. .................................................................
6. .................................................................

*Step 2: Discuss these with your people.*

*Step 3: List decisions in line with these values.*

1. .................................................................
2. .................................................................
3. .................................................................
4. .................................................................
5. .................................................................
6. .................................................................

*Step 4: Consider if you need to take corrective
action; i.e., if Steps 1 and 3 do not line up.
Actions to be taken:*

1. .................................................................
2. .................................................................
3. .................................................................

4. ...............................................................

5. ...............................................................

6. ...............................................................

**Action 91**   Check out the business values of your people, your suppliers and your customers. Are these the people we really want to build partnerships with?
If not, change them.

# ...AWARENESS

## 4.3 Image

### *– The management of the external identity of your business*

Image is the clothes you wear – what the world sees. It's what people say about you when you are not there! People make judgements about us all the time whether we like it or not. Our image can either be managed or left to chance. Successful companies are careful about maintaining a certain image with their customers. They leave nothing to chance.

One of the difficulties with image is that it is how others perceive us, not as we see ourselves. So how do we know? Well, you can ask people either informally or through your customer attitude survey. Hopefully, your external image will match with how you want to be seen, not like the following example:

| Self-Image | Customer Perception |
|---|---|
| • Innovative | • Stable |
| • Progressive | • Modern |
| • Professional | • Professional |
| • Customer focused | • Product focused |
| • Top end of the market | • Mid market |
| • Quality priced | • Expensive |
| • Confident | • Confident |
| • Future oriented | • Stuck in the present |

Clearly our friend has some image problems here!

---

### Example:–

"We developed a logo in 1984 and a letterhead. We reviewed this in 1990 after our design consultant produced some research, which showed that our image was that of an early '80s computer software business! At the time, logos were 'in' and the typeface modern. However, in six years we had grown and changed rapidly and our image did not match the current business personality, so we had to change it too..."

**– A Training Business**

---

### Example:–

"Company image had been a core feature with Ace from the beginning. Ace was chosen as a name for its alphabetical listing benefit and to represent being No 1, with the association of having a quality aim. The red diamond in the logo denotes quality and money – key elements of business success. The other card suits were not suitable, representing death, risk and romance!"

**– Ace Conveyors**

---

Image is not all about adverts. It is created by every message you send to the world. One delivery business gets its staff to answer the telephone on or before the first ring. Customer impression: 'this is a well organised outfit – I would trust them to perform.'

When I first started in business I called my house 'Melrose House'. I thought this sounded better to clients than 13 Arcadia Avenue!

---

## Example:–

One Hallmark Company dressed all its staff in blue overalls because its major customer, British Telecom, at the time was trying to convince the world that the image of dog mess and graffiti in its public phone boxes was simply not true. They wanted their cleaners to be visible and present the right image.

---

Image management is not about conning people into believing you are what you aren't, but simply ensuring that you are seen as being what you want to be... One company told me that they thought it unethical to manage their image, people had to take them as they found them. Frankly, as a customer I found them rude, arrogant and disorganised. I wonder what their other customers thought? How do your customers find you? What image do you portray to your world?

---

## Example:–

Some months ago my partner required some electrical work at home. She called an electrician from Yellow Pages. "I will be there at 6 o'clock." What time did he arrive? 9 o'clock. He walked straight over the carpet in the hall with mud spilling from his boots. "Can I borrow a ruler and a pencil" he enquired as he extinguished his cigarette in the sink.

She tried another company. "I will be there at 5pm." 5pm precisely, ding-dong. My God, she thought somebody turning upon time, this is unusual. This one sat on the doorstep, took off his boots and replaced them with carpet slippers from a suitcase. He also took out a white coat with the company logo on the back. He picked a clipboard, ruler and pencil from his case and said "Please show me the job." She told me: "I don't care if he has never wired a plug in his life: there is no way he will not get the job".

---

# ...ASSESSMENT

## 4.3   Image

**Tick here if this is true**
**for your business**

1.  *We manage our image very carefully in our business.*   ❑

2.  *Our customers perceive us as we want to be perceived.*   ❑

3.  *Our image creates new opportunities for us.*   ❑

4.  *People say good things about us.*   ❑

5.  *Our image creates trust and goodwill with our customers.*   ❑

6.  *Our image supports our business objectives.*   ❑

Less than 4 ticks and you need to take **ACTION...**

# ...ACTION

## 4.3   Image

***Action 92***   Write down the image that you wish to portray in your business. Use the checklist:

*Image Checklist*
*Your image covers:*
- *Name of firm*
- *Your name*
- *Address*
- *Personal appearance, clothes*
- *Car/vehicle*
- *Written correspondence*
- *Signage*
- *Logo*
- *Verbal correspondence, accent, small talk*
- *Where you are seen*
- *The way the phone is answered*
- *Prominence of your image*
- *Choice of colour in your livery*
- *Quality of type/word-processing*
- *Qualifications*
- *Membership of Associations*
- *Association with other parties/bodies*
- *Packaging of work*
- *Quality of paper and materials*
- *Personal manner*
- *Appearance of premises*
- *Spelling*
- *How quickly you respond to enquiries*
- *Ability to do what you say you will do – on time*
- *Type style on printed material*
- *Quality of finish on printed material*

(You know what's coming next by now don't you!)

**Ask** your key customers what image you portray. Ask them to do it in three words. This forces them to think.

**Take action** on the results; i.e., either crack open a bottle of champagne or train the telephonist, buy a new suit or change the letterhead!

**Action 93**   Get an independent opinion on the image your stationery and livery gives to your world.

**Action 94**   Try changing one aspect of your image and assess the impact.

**Action 95**   Employ an image consultant to look you over personally. (Get a good one.) What clothes and colours suit you best? Go on, I dare you...

**...AWARENESS**

# 4.4 Teamworking

Accepting the need for working as a team as the business grows is one of the most difficult lessons to be learnt by our Hallmarks companies. Many reflected that one of the key lessons of the past ten years has been the need to personally let go of the reins and trust and build a team.

The problem is that most business people are by nature both egotistical and independent, so trusting a team is not a natural process. The owner's energy and personal commitment eventually becomes the business' Achilles heel, because they cannot delegate and let go parts of their role. Yet the evidence is that it is very difficult to build a business beyond £1m single-handedly – so, if delegation is not addressed it can become a major obstacle to business development.

In talking with our Hallmark companies it appears that the problem is more than just a lack of technique (i.e., delegation skills) or training (i.e., all going on a teambuilding course together). It seems to be more about recognising your own strengths and weaknesses, the willingness to trust people and share power.

It was described by some as letting go, in terms both of the job itself, and psychologically. Here is a way that may help you let go gradually:

## Letting Go – a gradual approach

*Step 1:* Select the right person to delegate some of your work to.

*Step 2:* Identify a project or piece of your work which you can delegate.

*Step 3:* Agree objectives in outline with your selected person; e.g., reduce buying costs in admin by 10%. Or: keep customer service level at 92% satisfaction.

*Step 4:* Ask the individual to produce a one-page, bullet point action plan on 'how' they will achieve the objective. This has the benefits of:
- *Giving them personal ownership.*
- *Thinking for themselves.*
- *Conducting a mental rehearsal before committing to any action.*
- *Giving you an opportunity to check their thinking and provide any coaching input.*

*Step 5:* Once you are happy with the simple action plan give them the authority to implement it. Remember: interfere only once, and confidence is shattered. Set up a reporting line and let them come to you. People prefer to be judged by results, not conclusions.

Here are some tips from our Hallmarks companies about building a strong team:

- *Ensure your vision for the business is clear and shared by everyone.*
- *Build trust by keeping your promises and demonstrating that you trust people.*
- *Show genuine care for people.*
- *Banish competition, encourage collaboration.*
- *Encourage internal customer working.*
- *Provide leadership.*

So teamwork need not be a blockage if it is handled properly.

Finally, try to operate as a team, meet regularly, talk about important issues, consult and involve people, most of all learn to trust people.

# ...ASSESSMENT

## 4.4   Teamworking

**Tick here if this is true
for your business**

1.  *We enjoy excellent teamworking in our business.*   ❏

2.  *We collaborate and do not compete internally.*   ❏

3.  *We have learnt to trust each other in our business.*   ❏

4.  *People genuinely show care and respect for each
     other.*   ❏

5.  *We encourage people to play to their strengths.*   ❏

6.  *We have learned to let go.*   ❏

Less than four ticks means you need to take **ACTION...**

# ...ACTION

## 4.4   Teamworking

***Action 96***   Get an outside view about the quality of
teamworking in your business.

***Action 97***   Get your team together and ask them how
teamworking could be improved in your business.
List 10 actions to take:

*1.* ................................................................................

*2.* ................................................................................

*3.* ................................................................................

*4.* ................................................................................

*5.* ................................................................................

*6.* ................................................................................

*7.* ................................................................................

*8.* ................................................................................

*9.* ................................................................................

*10.* ..............................................................................

Keep your promises and demonstrate your
commitment and take action.

***Action 98***   Ask your team for feedback on your strengths and
weaknesses:

Strengths                    Weaknesses

*1.* ................................................................................

*2.* ................................................................................

*3.* ................................................................................

4. .........................................................................
5. .........................................................................
6. .........................................................................
7. .........................................................................
8. .........................................................................
9. .........................................................................
10. .......................................................................

Ensure you play to your strengths and either work on your weaknesses or delegate that part of your job to somebody who is good at it.

**Action 99**  Get your team together and ask them to provide each other (internal customers) with feedback to each other.

- *Identify blockages and problems.*
- *Agree actions to improve.*
- *Encourage them to talk more openly with each other about internal customer problems.*

**...AWARENESS**

4.5
Changing

# 4.5  Changing

## – Staying in tune

There is an interesting conundrum facing successful businesses. How to keep the recipe for success intact whilst adapting to change in their market?

Change in competitor activity or customer needs often provides the incentive to change the business, but what about when we want to change it? It appears that only crisis brings the energy to change; alternatively a 'new broom' – change of leadership will hasten the process.

Change is difficult. The 'Excellence' books were correct: "Emphasise quality, listen to customers, involve people, take dramatic action." These principles are confirmed by our own research. But those who preach the gospel of excellence don't deal with the deep seated sluggishness of resistance to change that pervades most companies. An inertia that has been called the 'psychopathology of the average', a mouthful, yet prophetic. We settle for mediocrity and don't change unless forced to by external influences. Many companies in the UK have made this an art form.

The 'Excellence' books caused a spur, and excellence became a destination sought by many. However, the world is changing too fast for excellence alone to provide a safe harbour. The trick lies in adapting the company to a constantly changing world. The challenge will never go away. Getting there is half the fun.'

---

> ## *Example:*
>
> The difference between getting there and the constant journey is epitomised in the quality area. ISO 9001 is the destination, an accredited standard, and a piece of paper. However the pursuit of quality improvements to products and services is a never-ending goal. It lasts forever.

So how do you stimulate change and make it stick?

Perhaps the most common cause of difficulty is that we under-estimate the complexity of change.

Change is a cultural process, it is not always rational. You need to change people's beliefs before you change their actions. This needs an understanding about how beliefs can be changed.

Your job is key to the change process in your company. You are the role model for others in your business. You need to spread your new vision to everybody, to act as a champion of change; Your people notice what you do and say, and so your actions must always support change.

Do you behave in ways that support the change you are aiming for?

Managers benefit from the use of a model in managing change effectively. Here is one used by a number of organisation, that have successfully managed change.

*Step 1: Assess the current situation.*

    A  *Assess problems and opportunities.*
    B  *Examine 'blind spots.'*
    C  *Select opportunities for action.*

*Step 2: Craft a new future.*

    A  *Develop a range of possibilities.*
    B  *Select a new future.*
    C  *Gain commitment to the new future.*

*Step 3:* *Make a plan.*

   A  *Brainstorm ways of moving from current situation to a new route.*
   B  *Develop a plan.*
   C  *Make the plan work.*

This process is well covered in the book *Managing Change and Innovation* by Gerard Egan. (University Associates Inc.)

Successful businesses are in a state of constant change whilst maintaining the integrity of the core product and service.

Change is a constant in today's world, but it starts with the beliefs and culture, not statistics and procedures.

# ...ASSESSMENT

## 4.5 Changing

**Tick here if this applies
to your business**

1. *We look forward to and welcome change rather
   than feel threatened by it.*                                    ❏

2. *We are good at making change stick in our business.*   ❏

3. *Our managers are good role models for change.*         ❏

4. *We are not afraid to make mistakes*                     ❏

5. *We first change people's beliefs and then their actions.*  ❏

6. *We support change with symbolic actions.*              ❏

Less than four ticks mean you need to take **ACTION...**

**...ACTION**

## 4.5 Changing

***Action 100*** Make change stick.

***Action 101*** Think about a change that you want to make to your business. Ask yourself, "How should I act as a role model to get the message across?"

Identify Major Change: How should I act as a role model to reinforce the change?

*1*.................................................................
*2*.................................................................
*3*.................................................................
*4*.................................................................
*5*.................................................................
*6*.................................................................

Remember what counts are actions not words.

***Action 102*** Change something in your business: meeting times, venues, dates, systems, anything. Sponsor the change and see what happens.

Things I could change in my business.

*1*.................................................................
*2*.................................................................
*3*.................................................................
*4*.................................................................
*5*.................................................................
*6*.................................................................

5.1
Spotting
opportunities

5.5
Increased
margins

**HALLMARK 5:
Competitiveness**

5.2
Revitalising
your
business

5.4
Work
'on' the
business

5.3
Creating
market
space

# Hallmark 5 – Competitiveness

## OVERVIEW:–

50% of our Hallmarks companies said that maintaining competitiveness is their major current challenge in the late '90s. We identified how successful companies retain their competitiveness.

*Hallmark 5:* *Competitiveness sets out the key principles and lessons in maintaining competitiveness in difficult trading conditions.*

In the first edition of this book we identified the challenges posed for the '90s by 250 European Managing Directors. The majority said the main one was: "Coping with increased customer demand for product, quality and service". This turned out to be a real underestimate. They did not foresee that deregulation and increasing globalisation would present such a threat (and in some cases opportunity) to UK businesses.

However many UK businesses have grasped the nettle and developed a real competitive edge. Companies that successfully create a competitive edge, continuously search for opportunities to be:

- *More efficient (improving the way they do things)*
- *More effective (adding new products or services, or improving their marketing).*

Hallmark 5 summarises these lessons for your benefit.

## ...AWARENESS

5.1
Spotting
opportunities

# 5.1 Spotting Opportunities

## *– To create a sustainable competitive edge*

Opportunities are the spark that ignites the competitiveness flame. When times are changing successful companies see opportunities to build their business, whilst the rest become overwhelmed by the threats.

Successful companies understand the difference between an idea (something they are interested in) and an opportunity (something that solves a customer's problem).

This section looks at creating new market opportunities (external) while section 5.2 considers opportunities to become more efficient (internal).

One of our Hallmarks companies summed it up: "Whenever we spend time with our customers trying to understand them and help them solve their problems we just seem to get lucky". They create their own luck.

Opportunities cannot be spotted sitting in a library or by conducting formal market research studies. You need to get out face to face with customers helping them resolve their problems.

However when the going gets tough it puts pressure on businesses and if they are not careful they become introspective and stop listening and taking calculated risks.

Our successful Hallmarks companies create new opportunities in the market place in several ways:

## 1 Conduct a customer attitude survey:

Ask your customers:

- *What you need to do to do more business with them?*
- *What is it that disappoints them about your business?*
- *How do you compare with your competitors and what can you do to improve?*

## 2 Problem-seeking/Problem-Solving

They use the Hallmarks processes identified in the first edition in 'Customerising'. Customer's problems become your opportunities, so find out where their pain is and fix it – fast.

## 3. Cross-selling

Successful companies ensure that they offer their customers their full range of products, services and extras, the aim is to optimise sales to existing customers. Share of customer spend becomes a key measure of success.

## 4. Identify the M.A.N.

The MAN means the person or people in the business with the money, authority and need for the product. Do we know who they are and have we targeted the right people?

## 5. Tap into your Network

Find out who the signposters and intelligence getters are in your industry. Who knows what's happening? Who is wired into the action? Find out and get to know them.

Spotting opportunities is an entrepreneurial activity that many businesses were once good at but may have lost the plot. Successful businesses work hard at creating opportunities to remain competitive.

# ...ASSESSMENT

## 5.1  Spotting Opportunities

**Tick here if this is true
for your business**

1. *We create enough profitable new opportunities to
   remain competitive.*  ❏

2. *We listen very carefully to our customers' problems.*  ❏

3. *We have well established intelligence networks that
   keep us updated on threats and opportunities.*  ❏

4. *We are good at translating new ideas into profitable
   opportunities.*  ❏

5. *We have an innovative team who create new
   opportunities.*  ❏

6. *We constantly reinvent our business.*  ❏

Less than four ticks and you need to take **ACTION...**

**...ACTIONS**

## 5.1   Spotting Opportunities

***Action 103***   Read *In the Company of Heroes* which covers creating opportunities in detail. (David Hall, Kogan Page, 1999.)

***Action 104***   Take yourself out of your normal business environment (visit the USA) and find out how other companies are responding to the threats and opportunities you face.

***Action 105***   Check how well you cross-sell by calculating your share of your key customers' total spend on your type of product or service. Plan to increase your share.

**...AWARENESS**

5.2
Revitalising
your business

## 5.2 Revitalising Your Business

### – *Improving internal efficiency*

Many companies have responded to competitive threats by making themselves move efficient, reducing their cost base and becoming lean and mean.

This does not mean they count paper clips or sack people. 'Downsizing' was never about efficiency improvements it was always about reducing head counts.

Businesses that once were entrepreneurial are now mature. They have established control systems and in many cases have become overmanaged with innovation and opportunity spotting being squeezed out of them. This ironically provides an opportunity to revitalise their fortunes, releasing much needed cash for reinvestment to rebuild competitive edge.

It is not easy but 'when the going gets tough, the tough...' (don't you just hate these patronising clichés? Maybe we should have a competition for the worst?)

We discovered that some Hallmarks companies have revitalised themselves using some of the following processes:

### Zero Based Budgeting

Most budgets follow this process:

1.  *Sales...*
2.  *Less Costs...*
3.  *What's left = profit (if you are lucky)*

This traditional budgeting approach builds in all the costs and assumptions you have made over the years.

To release cash and costs try this approach:

1. *Sales.*
2. *Profit; i.e., What do we want to create?*
3. *Costs; i.e., What we can afford.*

You estimate sales (1), then what profit you want (2), and finally that leaves the costs (3) you can afford.

Question every cost, asking is this really necessary?

Many businesses report taking out tens of thousands of pounds worth of costs using this method.

## Get '3' Quotes

This process involves getting 3 quotations from your existing major suppliers including accountants, banks, and material suppliers, etc.

Make them fight for your business, just as your customers do.

Again this can save you thousands of pounds in costs.

## Carry out a pareto on your stock (if you hold stock)

Calculate the 20% of stock items that produce 80% of your profitable sales, consider dumping the rest.

## Re-do your Strategy.

Analyse where you make money in terms of your products and markets. Cut out loss makers and focus on profitable lines.

## Outsource non-core activities.

Consider outsourcing those parts of your business that are non-core, this can significantly reduce costs and management time.

Our research revealed that many companies used these methods to revitalise their business. You can do the same.

# ...ASSESSMENT

## 5.2 Revitalising your Business

**Tick if this is true
for your business**

1. *We have outsourced non core aspects of our business.* ❏

2. *We regularly get 3 quotes from all our major suppliers.* ❏

3. *We have refocused our business where we make money.* ❏

4. *We have released sufficient cash to recreate competitive edge.* ❏

5. *We are as efficient as we can possibly be.* ❏

6. *Our business has a low cost base and is in good shape for the future.* ❏

Less than four ticks and you need to take **ACTION...**

# ...ACTION

## 5.2 Revitalising your Business

***Action 106***   Get 3 quotes from your key suppliers.

***Action 107***   Conduct a pareto on your stock.

***Action 108***   Conduct a zero based budgeting programme.

***Action 109***   Re-do your strategy focusing on where you make money.

***Action 110***   Get an outside view of the effectiveness of your business.

***Action 111***   Calculate some basic quality costs in terms of scrap/rework.

***Action 112***   Consider what you could learn from the most efficient companies outside your industry.

# ...AWARENESS

# 5.3 Creating Marketing Space

## – *Recreating competitive advantage by changing the way you compete.*

Successful companies create marketing space in order to break free from the competitive pack.

In order to do this they often reposition themselves compared to their competitors. There are three basic ways of creating this nirvana:

### *1. Copy substitutes.*

One way is to look at what products your customers are buying instead of yours and copy them. One Australian apple Company found that their customers were buying sugary sweets rather than apples, so they made apple segments look like sweets. Snack Apple is now doing very well.

### *2. Raise the Standards*

Derwent Valley Foods, manufacturers of Phileas Fogg snack foods, changed snack foods forever. Here are some of the characteristics they created:

- *Expensive looking and tasteful packaging that is distinctive.*
- *Unique products; e.g., Mignons Morceaux, small garlic croutons that are definitely a cut above potato crisps.*
- *Products made from natural ingredients without added chemicals.*

- *Products that are consistent.*
- *Products that cause friends to ask, "Where did you get these from, I love them?"*

## 3. Change the Appeal

Most products are purchased for emotional or rational reasons. Try changing your appeal.

For example, most training is sold on the basis that it is good for you, an act of blind faith. If you calculate the cost benefits to companies in *profit* terms, however, then they will often buy – i.e., change the appeal from emotional to rational.

Creating marketing space changes the rules in the industry and if done properly it can help you to gain competitive edge. It takes courage, imagination and a bit of entrepreneurial flair, but if you are being hammered on price and are struggling to make your profit aspirations you may consider it worth the effort.

# ...ASSESSMENT

## 5.3 Creating Marketing Space

**Tick if this is true
for your business**

1. *We enjoy high margins.*  ❏

2. *We do not force stiff price and source competition.*  ❏

3. *We have a clear, sustainable competitive edge.*  ❏

4. *We do not need to create marketing space in order
   to develop our business.*  ❏

5. *We are clear market leaders.*  ❏

6. *We can keep doing what we do the same way forever.*  ❏

Less than four ticks and you need to take **ACTION...**

**...ACTION**

# 5.3 Creating Marketing Space

***Action 113***    Review what substitutes your customers currently buy – what can you learn from this experience?

***Action 114***    Review with your customers how you could raise your standards and your prices.

***Action 115***    Consider changing the appeal of your product/service.

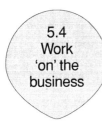

5.4
Work
'on' the
business

# 5.4   Work 'on' the Business

Successful business owners recognise that as well as working in the business they also need to work 'on' it.

As well as doing the job in a highly competitive world they need to improve the way they do the job.

The Japanese have a process for this, which they call Kaizen – continuous improvement.

The principles of working 'on' the business are straightforward:

1.  *You need to work on the business to improve your products and services in order to stay ahead of the competition.*
2.  *The best people to do this are everybody in the business who has vital information from experience of where the blockages and opportunities exist to improve your business.*
3.  *If you do not have a systematic proactive approach to this process it will not happen and the business will stay the same, even making the same mistakes over and over again.*
4.  *The process needs to be continuous, regular and action oriented.*

Here is how some of our successful businesses translate their principles into practice:

*   *Get your team together. Explain that you are all going to work on the business and you need their help and commitment.*
*   *Brainstorm areas for improvement, opportunities to reduce costs, improve efficiencies and make the business better. Try giving it a focus; i.e., improve our customer service or develop better*

*internal customer relationships or improve cross-selling.*
- *Turn the best idea into mini projects. Let the team appoint a leader and let people join, they then feel they can help.*
- *Agree initial actions and to meet in say 1 months time to report progress. Empower people to take responsibility and action.*
- *Provide support and encouragement during the month.*
- *Report successes and lessons learned and take the action.*
- *Continue the process.*

The overall aim is to involve everybody; and, most importantly, take actions.

A measure of success is the % of actions agreed that are actually taken. Aim for 80%+.

Our evidence is that if you encourage this process and are persistent you will continually develop your business and improve your competitiveness.

# ...ASSESSMENT

## 5.4   Work 'on' the Business

**Tick if this is true
for your business**

1. *Our people work 'on' the business producing
   results beyond expectations.*  ❏

2. *We have plans to improve our competitiveness.*  ❏

3. *We have developed a culture of continuous
   improvement.*  ❏

4. *We are as efficient and effective as we can possibly be.*  ❏

5. *Our people are well empowered and take responsibility
   often surprising me with the results they produce.*  ❏

6. *We seem to know what to do to improve, but we have
   difficulty in being persistent in taking actions.*  ❏

Less than four ticks and you need to take **ACTION...**

## ...ACTION

## 5.4   Work 'on' the Business

***Action 116***   Ask some selected staff for their ideas on improving your business.

***Action 117***   Carry out the working 'on' the business process outlined in this chapter.

***Action 118***   Ask people in your business what stops them taking improvement actions – fix it!

**...AWARENESS**

5.5
Increased
margins

# 5.5   Increased Margins

Here is your reward for implementing ACTIONS so far. Consider putting your prices up and improve your margins.

All of our successful companies charge premium prices.

Derwent Valley charges three times more for a standard packet of crisps. The message is clear! If you:

- *Customerise*
- *Partner*
- *Develop your personality*
- *Establish effective systems*
- *Are competitive*

You can charge higher prices and enjoy higher margins.

The reason is simple: successful companies provide what customers want. They add value to the product and develop a clear competitive advantage. Price becomes less important in this equation.

If you give people what they want they will pay you for it.

So, do *you* charge premium prices that reflect the quality of your business?

**...ASSESSMENT**

## 5.5   Increased Margins

**Tick if this is true
for your business**

1. *We charge premium prices to reflect the real benefits we offer our customers.*  ☐

2. *We give people what they want and they pay us well for it.*  ☐

3. *We have a significant price premium over our nearest competitor.*  ☐

4. *Price is not a real factor in our customer's buying decision.*  ☐

5. *Increases in price do not affect demand for our product.*  ☐

6. *We work smarter, not harder, for our money.*  ☐

Less than four ticks and you need to take **ACTION...**

## ...ACTION

## 5.5   Increased Margins

***Action 119***   If you have taken this book seriously and completed the actions diligently, put your prices up. You deserve it. Now open a bottle of champagne and toast yourself and your team. Well done!

6.1
Critical
information

6.5
Taking
action

**HALLMARK 6:
Systems**

6.2
Information
system

6.4
Key
indicators

6.3
Financial
control

# Hallmark 6 – Systems

---

**OVERVIEW**

All of the successful companies in our research had good systems, both formal and informal. Their systems added real value by providing good quality information to enable effective decisions to be made.

This chapter outlines the process of creating systems to support you and the business.

---

Many companies have control systems. Some will be more effective than others.

Our successful companies have excellent control systems but they also collect information to help improve the quality of decisions. They provide fast, accurate and relevant information so that people can take action to improve the business. They empower people through information.

This section shows how to empower people to make better quality decisions with the use of quality information.

# ...AWARENESS

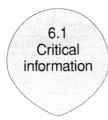

6.1
Critical
information

## 6.1 Critical Information

### – *Information needed to drive the business*

To see how the use of critical information supports successful businesses, let us eavesdrop on some discussions with two companies, A and B.

### Company A

*Q. What are your customer service levels?*
A. I don't know really. We don't get many complaints....

*Q. What management data do you get monthly?*
A. How much we have sold. We plan to get management accounts this year.

*Q. What information systems do you have?*
A. Do you mean computers?

*Q. What key indicators do you use?*
A. Key what?

*Q. How do you know whether you are successful or not?*
A. That's easy. When we are inside our overdraft limit!

## Company B

Q. *What are your customer service levels?*

A. We have 5 measures:
  - *4 week lead time for delivery.*
  - *98% delivery within 15 minutes of promised time.*
  - *96% delivery ex-stock within 48 hours.*
  - *All customer complaints handled same day.*
  - *Customers can place orders 24 hours a day.*

Q. *What management data do you get monthly?*

A. We have identified the key information we need to run our business. This is made available to those concerned within 5 working days of the month end. It includes:
  - *Monthly accounts by product/profit centre.*
  - *Sales platforms.*
  - *Customer services levels.*
  - *Key financial indicators.*
  - *Levels of repeat business.*

  This is all the information we need to manage our business.

Q. *What information system do you have?*

A. From receipt of customer orders right through payment. These are available instantly.

Q. *What key indicators do you use?*

A. We have ten indicators that take the pulse of our business daily. They include enquiries, orders, quotes, average order size, customer service levels, etc. This information is graphed and we can assess trends daily, weekly, monthly and year to date. We use this information daily to take action to develop our business. We could not run our business without this critical information.

Q. *How do you know how successful you are?*

A. We know daily from our key indicators.

Which of these two companies does yours most resemble?

Every business has critical information that helps managers make good decisions; without it they are effectively blind. It must be relevant to the key business issues; i.e., reams of computer printouts are useless.

Companies that rely on historical, outdated information are like car drivers doing 70mph looking through the rear window!

How do you establish what information is critical? Here is our approach.

*Step 1: Consider your customers.*

Why do they buy from you? What do they really want? The results of your customer attitude survey are the place to start.

For example, if quality and delivery on time were considered critical, your effectiveness on these factors becomes crucial to your success. So start with the key issues from your customer perception survey.

*Step 2: Consider how you get business?*

How effective is your business generating system? Measure it. It is critical if you are to build future business.

*Step 3: Key internal data, where are the real costs?*

One company found that labour accounted for over 60% of its costs. Consequently labour productivity and utilisation were critical to success.

*Step 4: Where do new opportunities exist?*

Where do you get information on customer, competitors and market trends? This is again critical.

---

### Example:

*Neat Ideas* has decided its key information needs are to provide data daily to every manager in the business. This allows them to improve the business daily. Their major competitors cannot assess this information until six weeks after the month end. Which do you think is going to survive long-term?

---

# ...ASSESSMENT

## 6.1 Critical Information

**Tick here if this applies
to your business**

1. *We have clearly identified the critical information we need in order to continually delight customers.* ❑

2. *We have examined how we get business and identified what information we require.* ❑

3. *Our internal analysis has revealed our major cost areas and other key issues we need to monitor.* ❑

4. *Information systems have been established to provide quick, accurate, critical information.* ❑

5 *Critical information is communicated to people to enable them to make effective decisions.* ❑

6 *Our critical information enables us continually to take the pulse of our business.* ❑

Less than four ticks means you need to take **ACTION...**

## ...ACTION

## 6.1   Critical Information

***Action 120***   Analyse your customer attitude survey. What are your customers' key needs in priority order? What does this tell you about the information you need to collect?

*Step 1: List customer needs in priority order.*

1. ..................................................................................
2. ..................................................................................
3. ..................................................................................
4. ..................................................................................
5. ..................................................................................
6. ..................................................................................

*Step 2: Decide how often you need to monitor how well you are meeting these needs.*

*Step 3: Decide how to gather the information to collect and monitor the key customer needs; e.g. Telephone sample for delivery performance daily.*

*Step 4: Feedback the information to people who need to take action.*

*Step 5: Use your information system to check the improvement has been made.*

***Action 121***   Examine how you get new business. What information do you need to gather to manage the business generating system? Does this information encourage you to act before problems occur or is your information so historical that it should be relegated to a museum!

| *Main sources of business* | *Information provided quickly Yes/No* | *Do we manage effectively? Yes/No* |
|---|---|---|
| 1. ......................... | | |
| 2. ......................... | | |
| 3. ......................... | | |
| 4. ......................... | | |
| 5. ......................... | | |
| 6. ......................... | | |

Act on the results of the above analysis.

**Action 122**   Examine your cost structure – where are the major costs? Are these monitored closely, daily or at least weekly?

| *Major Costs* | *Effectiveness of monitoring Excellent/Good/Poor* |
|---|---|
| 1. ......................... | |
| 2. ......................... | |
| 3. ......................... | |
| 4. ......................... | |
| 5. ......................... | |
| 6. ......................... | |

Take action on the results of the above analysis.

**Action 123**  Talk to your key people. Are they getting the information they need to run the business? Is their understanding of the prioritising the same as yours? Where are the blockages? Call in Dyno Rod!

*Information required to                  Your team's view*
*run your Business*
*(Your view)*

*1.* ..................................................................................

*2.* ..................................................................................

*3.* ..................................................................................

*4.* ..................................................................................

*5.* ..................................................................................

*6.* ..................................................................................

Act on any differences!

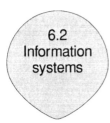

**...AWARENESS**

6.2
Information
systems

# 6.2   Information Systems

## – *Systems to enable good decisions to be made*

Most of our successful companies have good information systems, both informal and formal.

**Informal systems** are established by continual networking and customer contact.

**Formal systems** are computerised, providing key information quickly and accurately to decision-makers. This is seen as a potential source of competitive advantage.

> "If I know more about my customer's needs and my competitor's activity then we can compete effectively. Information is power in our business."
>
> **– Neat Ideas**

Accountants are often the instigators of formal information systems, so the financial data goes on to the computer first and if there is any capacity or interest then customer data may be collated.

It is possible to obtain excellent information systems off the shelf, which are customer orientated and fully integrated. Bisgen for example is a customer driven information system that fully integrates with the data and strategies set out in this book.

- *What information do we need to run our business effectively?*
- *How can we collect this information as efficiently and cost-effectively as possible?*
- *How can we set up a system that provides information when needed (rather than, say, 3 weeks after the month end)?*

# ...ASSESSMENT

## 6.2   Information Systems

**Tick here if this applies
to your business**

1. *We have excellent computerised information systems.*   ❑

2. *Our information systems support our key objectives.*   ❑

3. *We have all the information we need on our customers,
   markets and opportunities.*   ❑

4. *We use our information system to make
   effective decisions.*   ❑

5. *Our information systems provides us with a clear
   competitive advantage.*   ❑

6. *We are constantly upgrading and improving our
   information system.*   ❑

Less than four ticks means you need to take **ACTION...**

## ...ACTION

## 6.2    Information Systems

***Action 124***    Think about the key management decisions you have to make; e.g., price, priorities for expenditure, customers to focus effort upon. Does your existing information system enable you to make these decisions with real confidence? If it doesn't, change it.

| *Key management decisions* | *Quality of information available Excellent/Good/Poor* |
|---|---|
| *1.* ........................................................................ | |
| *2.* ........................................................................ | |
| *3.* ........................................................................ | |
| *4.* ........................................................................ | |
| *5.* ........................................................................ | |
| *6.* ........................................................................ | |

***Action 125***    Ask your key people whether they really have the right information to run your business. If not, do something about it.

***Action 126***    Ask for an outside view. Do you use state of the art computing hardware and software systems to support your business aims? If not, ask why not?

***Action 127***    Do you use a computer? If not, quickly book yourself on a keyboard course and get started.

6.3
Financial
control

# 6.3 Financial Control

## – *Sleep easy in your bed*

Successful growth businesses run the risk of growing out of control. This has been termed the Death Valley curve. The typical funds needed in a well controlled manufacturing company are about £25,000 of funding per every £100,000 increase in sales, whereas in a poorly managed company this can double up to £50,000 for every £100,000 in turnover. Turn your back on control for a mere few days, let alone months, and the cash requirements can escalate and sink your business. A useful read on the subject is *The Genghis Khan Guide to Business* by Brian Warnes (Osmosis Publications, London 1987).

Not understanding the difference between cash flow and profit and the dramatic increase in cash required for growth can bring disaster. Obviously there are exceptions to this rule. Any customer that collects cash before delivering the service or any business that collects cash faster than it pays out may not have a cash problem. For the rest of us the Death Valley curve can be a real threat.

The timing can also be problematic, as growth is usually driven by optimism and confidence. Cash flow problems can pour cold water over everything.

The first aim in financial control is to stay in business. This means managing cash flow, and understanding that gross margin – not sales – represents the true income of your business.

It also means being clear about the break-even point in your business, how much sales volume is needed to cover both fixed and variable costs?

Break-even is a key indicator and should be monitored closely.

---

## *Example:–*

A colleague recently visited a small business, which sold a technical engineering product that looked to have potential. The business had recently had a £400K cash injection. Their £25K per year sales people were selling £35K of products in total per month. The bank was getting nervous. Break-even wasn't known and when my colleague calculated break-even it was £85K per month! The bank was right to be nervous.

---

The essence of cash flow management is good systems to control debtors and creditors.

All of our growth businesses have a full-time qualified accountant. Deciding at what point to recruit a full-time internal accountant is difficult. If your sales are £1m+ get a full-time accountant tomorrow.

This simple advice will repay the cost of this book many times over in the first twelve months. Now you have your accountant, you don't need any more advice from me except this:

Your accountant will have a different perspective on your business than you. He will be cautious, pessimistic and careful. If you are a true entrepreneur you are the opposite – a risk taker. The point is that you need each other.

What value would an accountant add to your business? In my experience at least double his/her salary in year one!

Successful companies have the following:

- *Budgetary Control*
- *Job Costing.*
- *Pricing Policies.*
- *Profit Forecasts.*
- *Effective Borrowing Arrangements.*
- *Break-even Defined.*
- *Control of Gross Margins.*

Financial Control is a mirror image of your perception of your business; i.e., the better you understand it the faster you want key information.

The less you understand your business the less you see the need for good financial control information.

How do you see the need for financial information in your business?

---

## Example:–

"Financial control is vital to us operating in 10 regional divisions in the UK. Each one is a small business and each manager has sales and G.P. details weekly. They send it to Head Office to let us know how they are doing. We control our business weekly."

*– Ace Conveyor*

---

**...ASSESSMENT**

## 6.3   Financial Control

**Tick here if this applies
to your business**

1. *We understand the difference between cash flow
   and profit*                                                    ❏

2. *We have adequate funds to grow our business.*                ❏

3. *We have a qualified accountant in our team who
   attends and advises at all our important meetings.*           ❏

4. *We have excellent financial control systems that
   support our key objectives.*                                  ❏

5. *We calculate break-even and gross margins daily.*            ❏

6. *We have an effective cash flow forecast that enables
   us to manage our business effectively and avoid
   surprises.*                                                    ❏

Less than four ticks means you need to take **ACTION...**

**...ACTION**

## 6.3   Financial Control

*Action 128*   Employ an accountant full time if you don't have one! Especially if sales exceeds £1m.

*Action 129*   Produce a detailed accurate cash flow forecast for the next twelve months. Employ an external accountant to produce it for you if you do not employ one internally. (P.S. – Help them with the top line, the sales forecast.)

*Action 130*   Calculate break-even and gross margins by product/service and profit centre. Take action on the results.

$$\text{Break-even Turnover} = \frac{\text{Overheads}}{\text{Gross profit \%}} \times 100$$

(Gross profit = sales – variable costs)

Example:   $\dfrac{\text{Overheads £20,000 per month}}{\text{Gross profit 30 \%}}$

$$\text{Break-even Turnover} = \frac{20,000}{30} \times 100$$

$$= £66,667 \text{ per month}$$

*Action 131*   If you don't have them then ensure you have good financial controls within 1 month including budgets, cash flow, break-even and gross margins.

*Action 132*   Read *The Genghis Khan Guide to Business* by Brian Warnes (Osmosis Publications.)

**...AWARENESS**

# 6.4  Key Indicators

### – Taking the pulse

Key indicators take the pulse of the business on an ongoing basis. They monitor the important factors in the recipe for success for each individual business.

> "We monitor the key factors in our business daily and report the numbers to all our people. We monitor average order size, delivery performance, out of stocks, number of sales enquiries, and cash received. These factors tell us everything we need to know about our business."
>
> *Neat Ideas*

Successful companies decide what is important to monitor to maintain customer service levels. Less successful companies only appear to monitor internal issues; i.e., debtors, creditors, work in progress, etc.

Where should you start with key indicators? Start with the customer attitude survey results. What did your customers want from you? Make sure you have a key indicator on the key issues raised by your customers. If delivery was a key factor, monitor it. If quality was key, monitor it. Factors that are not important can be left alone. It's obvious really, but not many people do it.

---

Key indicators used by Danisco Pack, a leader in the packaging industry:

* Deliveries on time.

* Business from added valued customers (Design work)

* Supplier performance (JIT)

* Defect levels

* Overtime payments

* Wastage rates

---

Danisco Pack of Chesterfield monitors these 6 indicators weekly. Were you expecting them? The Managing Director says he now sleeps easier in his bed as the performance of each indicator has dramatically improved. Each indicator was plotted on a graph; plan versus actual weekly, monthly, and year to date.

Very often it is possible to develop 6-8 key indicators that take the pulse of your business. The most successful companies focus on customer-related indicators.

"If we get the customer indicators going in the right direction and maintain them, the numbers in terms of profit follow as if by magic." *Metro FM*.

A recent idea, we noticed that successful businesses now use trend indicators on a monthly basis and put trend lines through them using a technique called linear regression. This process smooths the curve caused by slight ups and downs. It gives a more helpful picture of trends over time. Ask your IT advisor for help in putting trend lines through your key indicators.

What key indicators do you need to run your business?

**...ASSESSMENT**

## 6.4   Key Indicators

**Tick here if this applies
to your business**

1. *We have identified our key indicators from a
   customer attitude survey.*  ❏

2. *We have a system for monitoring and reporting
   our key indicators.*  ❏

3. *Our key indicators are effectively communicated
   to everyone in our business who needs to know.*  ❏

4. *We have trends on our key indicators to monitor
   our progress continually.*  ❏

5. *We take action as a result of our key indicators to
   keep our business on track and moving forward.*  ❏

6. *We celebrate success when our customer key
   indicators tell us, and fix things fast when necessary.*  ❏

Less than four ticks means you need to take **ACTION...**

**...ACTION**

## 6.4 Key Indicators

*Action 133*   Conduct a customer attitude survey, if you haven't
completed one recently. Identify the key customer
indicators for your business. Set up a system to
monitor and report on them.

| *Key customer indicators* | *Systems established* | *Effective actions taken* |
|---|---|---|
| *1.* ........................ | | |
| *2.* ........................ | | |
| *3.* ........................ | | |
| *4.* ........................ | | |
| *5.* ........................ | | |
| *6.* ........................ | | |
| *7.* ........................ | | |
| *8.* ........................ | | |
| *9.* ........................ | | |
| *10.* ........................ | | |

*Action 134*   If you already have key indicators check them
carefully. How many customer indicators do you
have? If none go back to the previous action.

*Action 135*   Do you plot your indicators over time? Consider
putting trend lines through your indicators. If not,
consider it. This will give you a fabulous picture of
the progress and biography of your business.

*Action 136*   Check what happens to the key indicator
information. What actions result? Who does what?
Do things improve or change?

*215*

## ...AWARENESS

6.5
Taking
action

## 6.5   Taking Action

### – *Making Things Happen*

The major difference between the successful companies in our sample and the less successful ones is that the former TAKE ACTION. They do things, try things, and change things.

---

### *Example:*

There is a difference between knowing and doing. For example, at a seminar recently one of my colleagues asked the audience "Who are the most important people to your business?" The responses from 50 Managing Directors were instant and unequivocal. "CUSTOMERS", they almost shouted. The second question was, "So if customers are the most important contacts for your business how many of you have contacted them using a customer attitude survey in the last twelve months?" You've guessed the answer – none. Fifty say customers are the most important people yet nobody does anything about it... If our seven successful Hallmarks companies had been in the audience the answer would have been "SEVEN!!"

---

There is a difference between knowing and doing, taking action rather than theorising. The strange thing about business is that often people know what to do, yet they don't do it.

One of the key purposes of this book was to motivate people into action to do things, hence the model:

- *Awareness*
- *Assessment*
- *ACTION*

How many actions from this book have you taken so far?

Not only do actions improve or change the business, they indicate your intention to others. If customer service is a key issue and you jump in your car and take action on it, then this is a powerful message to everyone in your business.

One of my business contacts put it bluntly:

"If you want to stifle your business then talk about it, if you want to improve it then do something!

Start taking actions and you will get a domino effect. One action stimulates another and before you know where you are – you're well on your way. Sometimes you need to do one or two simple things first to build confidence. Once improvements are manifest you become more adventurous, but make sure you keep control.

This book may have taught you something or may even have motivated you but the rest is up to you. The incentive is that if you take the actions outlined in this book your business will change and improve. However, the decision is yours, it's your responsibility.

---

## Example:

An ex-boss of mine lit a candle before an assembled group of managers. He asked the audience to think the candle out – nothing happened. He asked them to plan the candle out – again nothing happened. He asked them to shout it out – nothing. Finally, he extinguished it with his fingers. "We can think and plan and shout about things, we can talk about them forever – but unless we do something (take action) nothing happens, ever!"

## ...ACTION

## 6.5   Taking Action

*Action 137*   If you have tried some of the actions so far then well done. On the way home tonight call in at your wine shop and pick up a bottle of champagne. Open it with your partner at home and treat yourself – well done!

*Action 138*   Enough of the fun. Back to the grind of making your business a real winner. Examine your track record to date. What actions have you taken? Why? What actions have you avoided? Why? Try out some of the actions you originally avoided. What have you learned?

*Action 139*   Consider the section on systems. What is the most important action you could take to move your business forward? Take it now.

# TOOLKITS

# Toolkit 1: Developing a Customer Commitment

This toolkit is designed to help you develop a customer commitment in your business.

---

**WHY CUSTOMERS QUIT**

| | |
|---|---|
| 1% | Die |
| 3% | Move Away |
| 5% | Develop Other Friendships |
| 9% | For Competitive Reasons |
| 14% | Are Dissatisfied with the Product or Service |
| **68%** | Because of a 'don't care' attitude to the customer. |

*– US and World News Report*

---

- *Photocopy this box, retype it, or get it nicely printed.*
- *Give it to your staff.*
- *Put it on the notice board.*
- *Talk to them about it.*
- *What does it mean to them and your business?*

## Taking Action

Developing a customer commitment means much more than basic "Have a Nice Day" customer care training. Your job is to get it into the 'hearts and minds' of your people, and this can take time and effort.

---

### DID YOU KNOW?

* The average business spends six times more to attract new customers than to keep existing ones.

* Only four out of 100 dissatisfied customers actually complain - 96 just go away.

* Dissatisfied customers tell on average between eight and ten other people... and one in five tells 20 others!

* It takes 12 positive incidents to make up for one negative incident.

* 70% of all people who complain will do business with you again if you sort out their grievance satisfactorily, and the figure rises to 95% if you resolve their problem on the spot.

---

## Developing a Customer Commitment

There is no single way of developing customer commitment in your business, but the following framework can be used to help assess where you are nowand provide a routre map to help you move forward. You should work through this and identify the combination of actions that suit your own situation. Experiment, try things, add your own ideas, and find a process that works for you.

---

## *Developing Customer Commitment involves:*

- Looking honestly at where you are now.
- Becoming a role model.
- Getting all your staff involved.
- Taking action.
- Monitoring your progress.

---

# Where Are You Now?

Take an honest look at your organisation, and complete the following questionnaire:

|  | Totally Disagree | | | | Totally Agree |
|---|---|---|---|---|---|
| 1. *Our customers re-confirm we are an easy business to buy from.* | 1 | 2 | 3 | 4 | 5 |
| 2. *Our senior managers are role models for customer commitment.* | 1 | 2 | 3 | 4 | 5 |
| 3. *We set clear standards in all our dealings with customers.* | 1 | 2 | 3 | 4 | 5 |
| 4. *Customers feature regularly in our management and team meetings.* | 1 | 2 | 3 | 4 | 5 |
| 5. *Senior managers are readily accessible to customers.* | 1 | 2 | 3 | 4 | 5 |
| 6. *We actively seek customer feedback on our performance.* | 1 | 2 | 3 | 4 | 5 |
| 7. *Feedback is passed on to our staff.* | 1 | 2 | 3 | 4 | 5 |
| 8. *We can provide 10 examples of commitment to customers in the past month.* | 1 | 2 | 3 | 4 | 5 |

9. *Everyone in our business understands that customers pay our wages.*    1    2    3    4    5

10. *Everyone in our business recognises and understands their role in satisfying customer needs.*    1    2    3    4    5

11. *Our staff regularly produce ideas to improve our performance.*    1    2    3    4    5

12. *Training plays a key role in improving our performance.*    1    2    3    4    5

13. *Everyone in our business understands how we are performing as a team.*    1    2    3    4    5

14. *Everyone in our business understands how he/she is performing individually.*    1    2    3    4    5

15. *We can provide 6 examples of 'delighted' customers in the past month.*    1    2    3    4    5

16. *Our office based staff have visited customers' premises.*    1    2    3    4    5

17. *We have developed real partnerships with our customers.*    1    2    3    4    5

18. *We are not seen as just one of their suppliers.*    1    2    3    4    5

19. *We understand our 'customers' customers'.*    1    2    3    4    5

20. *We regularly measure our performance as a supplier and our performance results are visible for all to see.*    1    2    3    4    5

Add up your total score to give a rating out of 100.

Your score is:       _____%

- *Photocopy the questionnaire above.*
- *Give it to your staff.*
- *Evaluate and compare the results.*
- *Do you have a true picture of what is happening?*
- *What ACTION do you need to take?*
- *What improvement targets are you going to set? (e.g., move from 56% to 70% by six months time...)*

# How Easy Are You to Buy From?

---

### *A TRUE STORY...*

A customer walks into an electrical hardware store with the intention (and the money needed) of buying a washing machine.

A fresh faced junior walks up to him and says, "How can I help you, Sir?" (courteous, friendly and warm as it said in the manual).

"I'd like to buy a washing machine, please" says the customer.

"Oh", replies the junior "the lady responsible for washing machines isn't here today. Er..."

There's a pause,

"...but we've a special offer on microwaves this week".

---

### *Introducing – the Sales Prevention Officer!*

This is the person in your business responsible for preventing customers from buying. It might not be his or her fault:

- *They may not have had the training.*
- *The systems may prevent them from selling.*
- *The structure might not help them.*
- *They might not have the authority or responsibility required.*
- *The incentive scheme may cause the problem.*

Whatever the reason, Sales Prevention Officers must be eliminated from your business.

They can lurk at any level of the organisation, in any department, and can emerge without you knowing.

### A customer driven business is one that is EASY TO BUY FROM

Select from these actions to begin the process:

- *Carry out a customer attitude survey as described in Hallmark 1.*
- *Ask your customers, "How easy are we to buy from".*
- *Get someone to ring your business, make an enquiry, or place an order.*
- *Why not do it yourself?*
- *Where are the blockages in your marketing and selling process?*
- *Ask your staff as well as customers, where are our sales prevention offices?*
- *How can we make it easier to buy from us?*

The things we need to eliminate sales prevention officers in our business are:

| Action | Who's responsible? | By When |
|---|---|---|
| e.g., *Joint Sales visit every qtr with reps* | *Sales Director* | *Year-End* |
| *1.* ................................................ | | |
| *2.* ................................................ | | |
| *3.* ................................................ | | |
| *4.* ................................................ | | |
| *5.* ................................................ | | |

226

# Customer Commitment Principles

"It's not what my staff see me doing they take notice of, it's what they see me not doing".

**– MD, Clothes Retain Group**

## Principle 1. Starts at the Top

Developing a customer commitment does not just happen, it has to be driven into the 'guts' of the business. The best place to start is at the top. Without commitment and drive from senior managers, it is unlikely to happen.

## Principle 2. Cannot be Delegated

Although it requires the involvement of everyone, the responsibility should not be passed on.

## Principle 3. Means Setting Standards

People must know what is expected of them to help, meet or exceed customer needs.

## Principle 4. Means Actions, Not Words

Senior Managers should set an example in deeds, not just words, and whenever possible set examples that are highly visible to all.

## Principle 5. Has to be re-inforced regularly

Customer commitment is an ongoing process and requires continuous reinforcement. It is not a nine-day wonder, and shouldn't be seen as a 'fad' by staff. Only start the process if you are prepared to drive it through.

# Toolkit 2: Customer Perception Survey

It's suggested you conduct a Customer Perception Survey in order to address the questions set out in the assessment sections in this book. It is conducted by telephone.

A Customer Perception Survey asks customers their views in a systematic manner. Here is the procedure for a tried and tested method.

*Step 1: Identify your key customers*

    *A: Which 20% of customers produces 80% of sales?*

    *B: Identify some 'lost' customers (your key customers will normally give you 'good news' – you want the full picture)*

    *C: Identify some customers you would like to do more business with in the future. Aim for 30-50 contacts in total.*

*Step 2: Write the following letter to your contacts:*

---

Dear (name),

In order to enable us to evaluate and improve the overall standard of the service (products) we offer and to ensure that we meet customer requirements at all times we would appreciate your help.

To do this we need to speak directly to our customers, seek their help and advice on our existing service (product) and over the next few weeks we will telephone you.

As a valued contact we hope you can help us to help you. Your views will be greatly appreciated.

Thank you.

---

*Step 3:* Determine what information you require and design your questions. Here are some we have prepared:

Q  What do you look for in a supplier? (probe to get at their detailed work)

Q  What disappoints you about suppliers?

Q  What improvements could we make in our service to you?

Q  What frequency of contact with suppliers do you prefer?

Q  How could we do more business with you in the future?

Design your own questions or change them into your own words. Each question can be followed with probes to establish real issues:

Q  Can you give me an example?

Q  Exactly what do you mean by that?

Q  What other things are important to you?

*Step 4:* Decide if you need to bring in a third party. [ref]

| | | PROS | | CONS |
|---|---|---|---|---|
| Own staff member | * | Knows your business well | * | Inexperienced at surveys, busy with own job |
| | * | Can sort facts from opinions | * | Customers may think you're selling |
| | * | Cheaper | * | Customers may be guarded in giving answers |
| | * | More experience | * | May be biased |
| Third party, i.e. a consultant | * | Objective - no 'axe' to grind. | * | Unfamiliar with the nuances of your business |
| | * | Experienced in undertaking such surveys | * | May obtain answers you 'want to hear'. |

*Step 5:* Telephone survey to the selected customers about seven days following the sending of your letter (Step 2).

Set out your questions on a sheet of paper leaving space for answers. Note the company's name on each form. Instruct the researcher to stick to the questions and to write answers verbatim – not to interpret the answers. Ask open questions.

*If the survey is conducted professionally and properly it will enhance your image with your contacts.*

*Sometimes businesses express concerns that customers will not talk and or will not respond honestly. Our experience with over 500 customers attitude surveys is that the problem is not getting customers to talk but to stop talking!*

*Remember they are more used to salesmen trying to sell them products than people genuinely interested in their views. "We only ever hear from them when they want to sell us something."*

Step 6: *Ask your customers to identify what is most important for each of the issues in Step 3. Then do the same with all the issues. Finally take each in turn and ask them to rate your business on a scale of 1-5:*

$$1 = Awful \quad 5 = Excellent$$

**Example:**

*"Mr Customer, you said delivery was your Number 1 priority. On a scale of 1-5 (5 being excellent), where would you rate us?"*

*"Do you mind if I ask whether our major competitors are above or below that rating?"*

Step 7: *Assess all the information collected.*

- *What was the most frequently mentioned issue?*
- *What are your customers' needs in priority order?*
- *How is the company perceived?*

*You should end up with an aggregate list of customers' needs and a rating of your performance compared to your competitors (see example).*

*You can see from the example that this quality of information provides a much better objective assessment of your business than guesswork.*

*Clearly the next step is to take ACTION to build on your strengths and address critical weaknesses. You may also have identified some new opportunities in your research, which you now want to take up.*

Example from one company participating in the basic research for this book. Customer needs (in priority order):

|  | Company Rating | Competitor Rating |
|---|---|---|
| 1. BS5750 Quality Assured | 9 | 3 |
| 2. Delivery on time | 5 | 8 |
| 3. Price | 7 | 7 |
| 4. Technical back up at weekend | 9 | 2 |
| 5. 3 week lead time | 3 | 10 |
| 6. Local representation | 7 | 6 |

Have a go yourself. What do you think they should focus on?

1. ...........................................................................................

2. ...........................................................................................

3. ...........................................................................................

4. ...........................................................................................

We would suggest:

1. *Emphasising quality assurance to new prospects.*

2. *Improving delivery performance to existing customers as quickly as possible.*

3. *Emphasising technical back-up to customers, particularly outside the working week.*

4. *Cutting lead times to 3 weeks.*

In addition customers said the following about them:

|  | % of customers |
| --- | --- |
| • *Difficult to place orders out of 9-5 times.* | *60* |
| • *Do not see sales contact often enough.* | *40* |
| • *Only see people when you want an order.* | *30* |
| • *Never return our calls.* | *20* |
| • *Quick to respond to enquiries.* | *60* |
| • *No named contacts.* | *10* |
| • *No worse than competitors.* | *20* |
| • *They never listen to us.* | *15* |
| • *Average-only customer service.* | *40* |
| • *Good at technical support.* | *80* |
| • *Good at solving our problems.* | *50* |

What do you think they should emphasise?

1. .................................................................................................

2. .................................................................................................

3. .................................................................................................

4. .................................................................................................

Perhaps:

|  | % of customers |
| --- | --- |
| 1. *Placing orders out of 9-5* | *(60)* |
| 2. *More sales contact* | *(40)* |
| 3. *Return calls more frequently* | *(20)* |
| 4. *Improve customer service* | *(40)* |

# Tookit 3: Problem-Seeking/Problem-Solving

This introduction to problem-seeking/problem-solving explains the principles behind the process and outlines how you and your staff could use the process to develop your business.

Talking to customers is great, listening to them is excellent, but an even better way to get information is to watch them.

You and your staff should spend time with customers "at the sharp end", to find out:

- *What do they do with your product or service?*
- *How do they use it?*
- *Why do they use it that way?*
- *Who are their customers?*
- *How does it help them help their customers?*

Being there, not just talking about being there, can help you to help them.

---

"We accompanied one of our customers on a site visit when they were installing one of our replacement parts in a tractor. We soon found that our packaging was too bulky for them on site, and that the accompanying installation instructions were useless. The engineers said they'd grumbled regularly to their boss about them, but this had never been passed on to us.We sorted it quickly."

**– *Sales Engineer, Engine Component Distributor***

---

Understanding customer needs means getting into and understanding their world.

The keys that unlock this door are:

- *Watching customers at the sharp end.*
- *Asking the right questions.*

"What customers say they want, and what they really need can often be two completely different things".

Finding out about their real needs requires attention of the individual, and sometimes help identifying those real needs.

One of the problems of asking customers what they want is that they may tend to answer from their own blinkered perception. They'll say they want "it" faster, a little better, cheaper, a higher specification, etc.

When they are asked, many customers will not suggest dramatic or surprising ideas, but simple incremental improvements.

Another key principle in understanding customers to really help customers, we must dig deeper. Understanding customer needs doesn't mean just asking customers what those needs are, it means:

- *Knowing their goals and aspirations.*
- *Understanding their real problems.*
- *Knowing how you can help them achieve these goals and overcome their problems.*

It's called Problem-seeking/ Problem-Solving.
So, how can we do this?

## ASK THE RIGHT QUESTIONS

There are two types of questions that help you really understand customer needs.

1. *Problem-seeking.*
2. *Follow Up.*

The kind of questions which will encourage customers to talk about problems and concerns include:

- *What improvements would you like to see in your business?*
- *If you could change one thing in your business, what would it be?*
- *What is causing you most difficulty right now?*
- *What would have the biggest impact on your business?*
- *What's stopping you achieving your goals?*
- *What's stopping you moving forward?*
- *What's preventing you buying?*
- *What irritates you about suppliers?*
- *How can we make it easier for you to buy?*
- *What problems have you had in the past?*

Once a customer has flagged up an issue, your task is to:

- *Help him or her examine the problem in detail.*
- *Fix the problem.*

## Examine the problem in detail

Once the customer has identified the problem you need to ask further questions and, above all, listen carefully to the answers.

## Fix the problem

Ask the customer, "If I could help you find a way through this, would you be interested?"; Or: "If I could help you sort this out, would you be happy?"

Then either:

a) offer your solution (if it is a problem where you can help), and arrange to implement the solution fast; or:

b) suggest that you get back to them within a specified time limit, (2 hours, 2 days, 1 week – whatever), when you will be able to provide a solution.

If you cannot solve the problem yourself, use your network. If your network is nourished and up to date you are almost bound to know someone who can help. Call in favours from the past and secure help on behalf of your customer. Follow up by contacting your customer within the specified time limit and presenting the solution. Remember, problem-seeking + problem-solving = a friend for life.

## The Problem-Seeking/Problem-Solving Process

Use the following four-step process to build business with either existing or potential clients:

1. *Build trust.*
2. *Consider possibilities.*
3. *Craft an agenda.*
4. *Fix it fast!*

*Step 1:* Build trust

*You can build trust with your customers by:*

- *Showing respect for your customers; their time; their space; their views and opinions, their products or services.*
- *Treating customers as individuals.*
- *Dealing with them in a friendly, yet professional manner.*
- *Disclosing things about yourself. Show them that you are human too.*
- *Listen carefully to what they have to say.*
- *Asking relevant questions to find out more, rather than assuming you 'know it all'.*
- *Making sure that you do whatever you say you will do, and doing it within the agreed time.*
- *Being genuine. This means admitting errors and mistakes, telling the truth at all times, and never, ever making promises you can't keep.*

*Step 2:* Consider Possibilities

*Having agreed on the problem, the next step is to jointly consider the solution. For example, the problem is:*

*The customer needs to receive information faster from you so that she can plan production more effectively.*
*The possibilities are:*

1. *You identify a manager who can liaise with the customer on a daily basis.*
2. *You install an on-line computer modem to send data quickly.*
3. *You arrange regular meetings with the customer, maybe once or twice a week.*

*Discuss the possibilities with the customer and involve them in the decision making process. Undoubtedly, if customers feel that they have some 'ownership' of the agreed solution, they are much more likely to be committed to the plan and will work harder to ensure that the plan actually works in practice.*

*Step 3:* Craft an agenda

*Once you have agreed a possible solution or way forward, the next step is to agree, jointly with the customer:*

- *Who is going to do what?*
- *What is the time scale?*
- *Who pays for what?*

*Step 4:* Fix it fast!

*Even if you have agreed a timescale of a week, try to fix the problem in a day. Surprise, impress and delight your customer! Fast, effective response is the key to success in the process of problem-solving and problem-seeking, and this is particularly true if you are trying to create a relationship with a new customer who has given you your first opportunity to show what you can do. Work all night if you have to, but fix it fast.*

## Action Plan

To improve our effectiveness in problem-seeking/problem-solving, we need to:

1. ............................................................................................................

2. ............................................................................................................

3. ............................................................................................................

4. ............................................................................................................

5. ............................................................................................................

6. ............................................................................................................

# Toolkit 4: The Business-Generating System

## Introduction

The Business Generating System is a sales and marketing system, which combines Information Technology techniques with the style of marketing used by fast-growth, successful businesses.

It is of benefit to firms where there is the potential for repeat or referred business, individual order values are significant and buying decisions are 'considered,' not 'impulsive'.

## I.T. in Sales & Marketing

The use of computer based sales and marketing systems in business is growing at 30% per annum in the UK.

MSP (Marketing and Sales Productivity Systems) provide the following benefits.

- *increased sales*
- *more effective resource utilisation*
- *automatic collection of market information*

Research by Shaw Consulting in 1990 indicated that users of MSP systems expected a 7% turnover increase between 1990-92. Evidence from research in the United States shows those early adapters of MSP system gained sales increases of 10% to 30%.

The Business Generating System uses the latest 4GL (4th generation language) programme which combines the benefits of database reporting, automation of administration systems management (hence time saving) with user friendliness and adaptability.

# Relationship Marketing

All of us are exposed to over 50,000 selling messages every year. The effect is that people are becoming hardened and conventional advertising less effective.

The message from successful companies demonstrates the strength of the caring and personal approach – the present economic climate has heralded the advent of Relationship Marketing; i.e., Hallmarks, as opposed to marketing by numbers.

- *'Problem-seeking/Problem Solving'*
- *'Networking'*
- *'Friend for Life'*

The usual situation is that the top person in any firm is naturally 'good' at relationship marketing, either deliberately or instinctively. The barrier to growth usually happens when the sales demand begins to exceed the compass availability of the top person. Stagnation and even decline results if the firm is a Relationship Marketing culture and does not empower other senior employees with the same skills and desire to use the technique.

# Where the Business Generating System counts

The Business Generating System enables firms to make the break from potential stagnation. The I.T. component makes time input more productive; resource investment more accountable through live management reporting, and data handling easier. The underpinning philosophy expands on these benefits to provide a winning marketing formula for the 1990s. Quantifiable and easily-monitored, it is a refreshing change from the aggressive and impersonal technique that spreads demand, exceeds supply and reduces true competition, to the detriment of all.

# How the Business Generating System Works

The success of the Business Generating System (BGS) is based around the following fundamental points:

## *Fits with your focus/direction*

BGS does not try and impose on you a new way of doing things, but recognises what works for you and builds on these strengths.

## *Focuses your objectives*

Included in the BGS is a marketing review to make sure business development efforts are focused and in pursuit of clear business objectives.

## *Links marketing to financial targets*

Using BGS the volume and type of marketing activity is planned to generate the level of business needed to meet your financial targets.

## *Measurable outcomes – Key indicators*

The computer database at the heart of BGS enables management to monitor outcomes from its investments and review key indicators on the performance of individuals, methods, products and the entire business. Quite simply, this means visible business health, knowledge of the areas of real value and the ability to use such information to stay ahead of competition.

# Key Indicators

The Business Generating System produces 'key indicators' to show management the health and effectiveness of a business. Note that these key indicators occur upstream of conventional financial indicators thus giving firms forward visibility of financial performance.

| *INDICATORS* | *PURPOSE* |
|---|---|
| *Business Plan Indicators* | *Defined from the chosen plan, and used to track effectiveness of the plan.* |
| *Customer Delight* | *% of 'demand led' new business that is indicative of sustainable competitive advantage* |
| *Working Platform Value* | *Level of quoted business necessary to sustain sales platform at operational target.* |
| *Conversion Rate* | *Barometer of change and marketing effectiveness.* |
| *Sales Platform plan* | *Order book value to meet business objectives.* |
| *Sales Invoiced* | *Determinant of production effectiveness in conjunction with Sales Platform.* |

# Toolkit 5: Searching for Opportunities to Improve Competitiveness

Opportunities to improve competitiveness can come from:

## Talking and listening to customers

- *What do they look for in suppliers?*
- *What do they want, they are not getting?*
- *How do they rate you on specific issues compared to competitors?*
- *What are you good at that customers like?*
- *How could you improve your performance?*
- *What could/should you do that competitors aren't/can't?*
- *What would an 'ideal' supplier do, look like, sound like etc?*

## Your own standards/ideas

- *What would your ideal supplier offer?*
- *What do you know you need to do better?*
- *How can you leverage what you're good at to become even better?*

## Environmental changes

- *What changes in the environment provide opportunities to create competitive advantage?*

## Competitive Assessment

Here is a toolkit to help you look at your competitors and establish how they rate in the following activities. Get your team together and review your competitors' performance by answering the following questions.

Score on a scale of 1-5 as follows:

| 1 | 2 | 3 | 4 | 5 |
|---|---|---|---|---|
| *Never* | *Sometimes* | *Quite Often* | *Usually* | *Always* |

|  | Us | The Best | The Best at this is: |
|---|---|---|---|
| *Deliver on time.* | ❏ | ❏ | ............. |
| *Provide a consistent quality product or service.* | ❏ | ❏ | ............. |
| *Delight their customers.* | ❏ | ❏ | ............. |
| *Continually improve what they do.* | ❏ | ❏ | ............. |
| *Actually do what they say they can do.* | ❏ | ❏ | ............. |
| *Are easy to buy from.* | ❏ | ❏ | ............. |
| *Respond quickly to customer enquiries.* | ❏ | ❏ | ............. |
| *Provide innovations and ideas.* | ❏ | ❏ | ............. |
| *Solve customer problems quickly.* | ❏ | ❏ | ............. |
| *Have high repeat business levels.* | ❏ | ❏ | ............. |
| *Provide outstanding product/service support.* | ❏ | ❏ | ............. |
| *Don't compete on price.* | ❏ | ❏ | ............. |
| *Get the best from their people..* | ❏ | ❏ | ............. |
| *Get a lot of business referrals.* | ❏ | ❏ | ............. |

*Win customers from their competitors.* ☐ ☐ ...............

*Promote themselves well..* ☐ ☐ ...............

*Have excellent front line staff.* ☐ ☐ ...............

*Recruit the best people.* ☐ ☐ ...............

*Provide an excellent after-sales
service.* ☐ ☐ ...............

*Produce a profit.* ☐ ☐ ...............

Now rate your own organisation honestly on the same scales:

*Deliver on time.* ...............

*Provide a consistent quality product or service.* ...............

*Delight our customers.* ...............

*Continually improve what we do.* ...............

*Actually do what we say we can do.* ...............

*Are easy to buy from.* ...............

*Respond quickly to customer enquiries.* ...............

*Provide innovations and ideas.* ...............

*Have high repeat business levels.* ...............

*Provide outstanding product/service support.* ...............

*Don't compete on price.* ...............

*Get the best from our people.* ...............

*Get a lot of business referrals.* ...............

*Win customers from our competitors.* ...............

*Promote ourselves well.* ...............

*Have excellent front line staff.* ...............

*Recruit the best people.*                    ...............

*Provide an excellent after sales service.*                    ...............

*Produce a profit.*                    ...............

---

These are the areas we need to work on to improve our competitiveness:–

1. ..................................................................................

2. ..................................................................................

3. ..................................................................................

4. ..................................................................................

5. ..................................................................................

---

If you cannot answer the previous questions, then consider the following activities:

- *Carry out a customer attitude survey (see Hallmark 1).*
- *Undertake a formal review of competitor's performance.*
- *Visit Trade Shows.*
- *Obtain your competitors' brochures/promotional materials.*
- *Look honestly at your own business.*
- *Talk to key influencers in the industry; i.e., those 'in the know'.*

# A Competitive Checklist

Here are some issues you may wish to consider to stimulate ideas about areas which offer scope for creating competitive advantage:

- *Ease of placing orders.*
- *Good telephone response to enquiries.*
- *Speed of response to enquiries.*
- *Speed of providing quotations.*
- *Solving customer's problems.*
- *Rapid response to queries/concerns.*
- *Personal sales style - friendly, helpful, and effective.*
- *Lead time.*
- *Delivery reliability.*
- *Communication during order processing.*
- *Technical know how/ability.*
- *Advice and guidance.*
- *Regular ongoing communication with customers.*
- *Delighting customers with extraordinary responsiveness to their needs.*
- *Pricing policy.*
- *Uniqueness of product/service.*
- *Quality of product/service.*
- *Range/availability.*
- *Packaging.*
- *Reputation.*
- *Quality of staff.*
- *Image.*
- *Promotional activities.*
- *Guarantees.*
- *After-sales services.*

Identify areas where you can develop a competitive advantage and then begin work on them. Remember, it is no good being significantly better than competitors at something if customers do not place a value on this.

> Competitive Advantage must be based on what customers want and will pay for.

As a result of this toolkit, define, or redefine your competitive advantage.

| Our competitive advantage should be made up of the following distinct bundle of skills, methods and practices:– | |
|---|---|
| Elements | Action needed to improve and develop this |
| | |

# Appendix: The Research Programme

## Introduction

There are about 40,000 British companies which employ between 50 and 5,000 people. In fact, 70% of non-government employees work for enterprises (both incorporated and unincorporated businesses) employing fewer than 500 people. Reliable statistics about such companies are hard to come by, but it is estimated that this sector generates around 30% of gross domestic product.

However, there may be another 1m or more enterprises employing only 1-50 people with ambitions to develop their business.

Despite their importance to the U.K. economy, small independently owned businesses receive remarkably little attention. Even in the United States, which celebrates its independent sector, they are the 'silent majority'. Also, despite the efforts of the National Federation of Small Businesses and other organisations, and the appointment within the DTI of a Minister for Small Businesses, they lack comprehensive and authoritative representation in the U.K. and have very little voice.

With the shake-out of middle-management, white collar workers in two recessions, and the trend to downsizing in large organisations, the 1980s fuelled the growth of the private sector. Over the past decade there has been a net gain of 373,000 businesses registered for VAT, many of them tiny, but an increase nevertheless of nearly 30%. Still, there is much to do if our independent companies are to compete effectively at home and abroad in a tough business climate with high costs of capital.

What can be done to support ambitious businesses?

Clearly the support they need is different from that of the start-up enterprise or the multi-national corporation. What do they need?

# Background

Allan Gibb, Chairman of the Foundation for SME Development at the University of Durham, and I sat in a bar one evening swapping prejudices. We were surprised when we agreed on something (Allan is a professor and I am a businessman). We seemed to be asking the same questions. Is marketing taught in a relevant way to small independent business? Do small businesses really need to know how ICI develop marketing plans? (It is not uncommon at some business schools to find independent businesses being taught by bank managers using Jaguar Cars as an example!)

We wondered how:

- *Independent businesses really grow (never mind the theory!).*
- *Could we support independent businesses in their development?*

These questions provided the basis for the research which eventually led to this book.

We decided to put my money where Alan's mouth was and sponsor some research. British Coal Enterprise Ltd. and the Regional Enterprise Unit of the Department of Employment also sponsored the work.

The objectives of our research collaboration were:

- *To find out how companies really grow and develop.*
- *Decide how we could most effectively support the development process.*
- *Develop some case studies of good practice, which might be used by trainers and counsellors working with clients.*

# Method of Research

The first step was to recruit a full-time researcher. We decided to go for somebody who was not a marketing expert (they may only confirm their own beliefs).

We asked our respective networks to identify some successful companies and came up with 80 who fitted our requirement. These were drawn from service, manufacturing and the retail sector and from the North East and South Yorkshire to reduce regional bias. They all had a track record of sustainable growth and profit and eventually. 30 companies agreed to be involved in our research.

The research was divided into three stages:

### Stage 1. Fact-finding Interview

The first stage was a fact-finding interview with the managing director. These interviews were recorded and transcribed. The objective was to build up a factual company profile from forty questions. For example: What sort of company? How old? How many employees? How many products? Which markets do they serve?

Once this stage was complete and the interviews transcribed, the transcript was analysed for critical instances. For example: "We increased our sales that year threefold." These were recorded for the next interview...

### Stage 2. The Process Interview

This focused on the process of development identified from the first interview. How did sales increase threefold? The second stage interviews were much more open-ended: trying to understand the real process of development. The interviews probed areas of real interest, lasting 3-4 hours on average and we recorded and transcribed them. The transcripts were typically 40 pages of A4 typing.

Going from a factual first interview to an open-ended format generated lots of data. Many questions might have seemed naive to the business people, but the researcher was trying to act like a sponge - absorbing information without any preconceived ideas of the answers. The use of open questions allowed the collection of qualitatively rich data.

This method is a good way of surfacing real issues, which might never get aired using a structured process. Each experience was unique.

## Stage 3. Analysis

The next stage was to analyse the mass of data we had gathered. 30 companies x 40 A4 pages = a paper pile about 2 feet high.

After the second round of interviews we began to analyse the reams of data. We first looked for critical instances and blockages to growth. These were plotted on graphs against sales and profit trends. We went back yet again to the companies for explanation of peaks and troughs. Why did sales increase here? What did you do to make it happen? We then classified the companies into composite groups such as Manufacturing and Service, Exporters and UK only, etc. In order to analyse them (comparing and contrasting) we needed to establish criteria for success against which to assess our companies. *What is success?* How can it be defined?

We considered many standard tools for analysis; e.g., turnover-per-employee and capital expenditure-per-head. We finally decided on growth by number of employees and years' trading. We defined success as those trading less than 10 years, employing more than one hundred people, with a consistent profit and sales record. We feel this is defensible given our original hypotheses. Clearly, other people will want to use different success criteria – there is no unique answer.

We found in our analysis of the results that the seven really fast growth companies had many things in common – not least the type of managing director. Our researcher commented that if she shut her eyes in the seven companies she could be talking to any one of them! Their beliefs, attitudes and behaviour were almost identical. We also found that the process by which they developed was also remarkably similar. They all have the same hallmarks... Hence this book.

Both Allan Gibb and I believe the research has gone some way to challenge traditional textbook marketing based on large company models. But we are biased. Judge for yourself. Read the book.

For those of you wanting more details of the research process, contact **Dinah Bennett at The Foundation for SME Development at the Univeristy of Durham, Mill Hill Lane, Durham DH1 3LB.** The research was initially presented to the 1991 UKEMRA Conference in Manchester and the European Foundation for Management Development Conference (EFMD) in Barcelona later that year.